BILL DONAHUE

HOW TO LEAD A LIFE-CHANGING SMALL GROUP

How to Lead a Life-Changing Small Group

Published by HarperChristian Resources, 3950 Sparks Drive SE, Suite 101, Grand Rapids, MI 49546, USA.
HarperChristian Resources is a registered trademark of HarperCollins Christian Publishing, Inc.

Requests for information should be sent to customercare@harpercollins.com.

ISBN 978-0-310-18356-3 (softcover)
ISBN 978-0-310-18360-0 (ebook)

HarperChristian Resources titles may be purchased in bulk for church, business, fundraising, or ministry use. For information, please e-mail ResourceSpecialist@ChurchSource.com.

HarperCollins Publishers, Macken House, 39/40 Mayor Street Upper, Dublin 1, D01 C9W8, Ireland (https://www.harpercollins.com).

This resource is adapted and updated from *Leading Life-Changing Small Groups* (third edition), Copyright © 2012 by Bill Donahue and Willow Creek Association.

Art Direction: Ron Huizinga
Cover Design: Tammy Johnson
Interior Design: Inside Out Design

Dedicated to every leader who has answered the call to serve the kingdom of God by guiding a small group of fellow seekers toward maturity in Christ. May Jesus reward you for your faithfulness and unwavering devotion to your ministry.

CONTENTS

PREFACE

Welcome! This manual has been designed by small-group leaders, group pastors, and ministry leaders to help you as you lead your small group. It is a reference guide and working document for your ministry, providing the information and resources you need to lead a transformational small group in which life change is the norm, not the exception.

HOW TO USE THIS RESOURCE

You'll find that *How to Lead a Life-Changing Small Group* is organized in a way that anticipates your questions, making it easy for you to find the information you need when you need it. It's also designed with a lot of common sense, with each section leading into the next. Using the tools in this book, you'll be able to lead the kind of small group that turns participants into fully devoted followers of Jesus Christ.

Throughout the material are places for you to interact, enter your own thoughts, or develop a strategy for some aspect of your ministry. Take the time to engage the material when prompted.

HOW THE MATERIAL IS STRUCTURED

Chapter 1 begins with the underlying principles and values of biblical community, giving you a vision for group life. Beliefs give rise to actions. What you believe about community, small groups, discipleship, and leadership in the body of Christ will determine the nature of your ministry efforts and success. This section provides you with the core for developing a thriving and exciting ministry.

Chapters 2 and 3 strike at the heart of a successful small group: your personal leadership. Trained, gifted, and passionate leaders form the backbone of a small group ministry intent on developing fully devoted and fruitful Christ followers. Here you will examine the spiritual life, responsibilities, and character of the small group leader.

Chapter 4 focuses on the successful development of other leaders through apprenticing. Shared leadership is the biblical norm; it is not simply the responsibility of a few paid staff members. You will invest in the rising generation of disciples as you identify, challenge, motivate, and equip people who will become future life-changing group leaders.

Chapter 5 teaches you how to grow the best environment for group life. After you shape and cast a biblical vision for your ministry, understand your role as a leader, and commit yourself to developing potential leaders, you can focus on the inner workings of your group. Here you'll find guidance for forming your group, shaping its vision, establishing ground rules and a covenant, and understanding healthy communication patterns.

Chapters 6 and 7 walk you through the skills and information needed to conduct life-changing meetings—from designing a meeting to using great questions, handling conflicts, building relationships, and leading dynamic discussions. Meetings are the most catalytic aspect of your ministry—a prime opportunity to gather, build momentum, deepen relationships, and accomplish your purpose. You will also learn important factors for leading online groups.

Chapter 8 helps you gain essential feedback to measure progress and make adjustments as you lead. The tools here will give you insights into your own leadership growth and effectiveness, as well as information about how the group is doing.

Chapter 9 has resources to help you become a shepherd and help your people become a caring group. You will learn to encourage members and create a nurturing environment where members find rest for their souls, prayer for their needs, and healing for their spiritual and emotional wounds. You will learn how to lead when a group member is in crisis or needs some "intensive care" beyond what the group members and you can normally handle.

Chapter 10 lays out how to help the group make an impact with others outside the group. You have the privilege of extending the kingdom of God beyond your group by reaching out to others who have yet to experience the fullness of true community in Christ. You'll learn how to connect others to group life, explore ways to serve others in your world, and find resources for having conversations with spiritual seekers.

Finally, there are three appendices at the back of this book: "Common Categories of Small Groups," "Relationship-Building Exercises," and "Studying the Bible Together."

So dig in and get ready for the adventure of your life—leading a life-changing small group that is producing followers of Jesus Christ who are dedicated to one another and are committed to building God's kingdom together.

INTRODUCTION

My family was preparing to eat dinner and wanted a couple of creative questions to raise the discussion energy beyond "How was your day?" and "What's going on this weekend?" My wife smiled and reminded us there were dozens of icebreakers and discussion starters in the book *Leading Life-Changing Small Groups* that we have used with small groups over the years. My son grabbed the book off the shelf and skimmed through about one hundred ideas listed in the chapter on Leading Life-Changing Meetings, and soon we had several options.

But then he said to me, "Hey, Dad, when did you write the first edition of this book? This third edition is dated 2012."

"I think it was 1996," I said.

He did the math and exclaimed, "So this year, 2026, will be the 30th anniversary! That's cool! Maybe it's time for a fourth version—a 30th anniversary edition!" We all smiled, and I decided to pitch the idea to my publisher. The rest, as they say, is history. What you are holding is the outcome of that conversation, now titled *How to Lead a Life-Changing Small Group.*

As I pondered reaching this publishing landmark, grateful for God's grace in making it accessible to so many people globally, I realized a lot has taken place in our world over the past thirty years. There have been many changes in the church and "small-group world" as well. To be sure, some things never change, especially the fundamentals. American baseball, for example, has changed over the decades—updated rules, huge salaries, new teams, more baseball parks, creative broadcasting media, and the rise of baseball as a corporation—but the basics have remained the same. A player still has to be able to throw, catch, hit, and run.

Small group leadership fundamentals—such as reading the Bible together, guiding a prayer time, engaging in meaningful discussions, caring for one another through times of grief and suffering, and having a mission—remain core practices for any good leader. But there have been important changes in the past thirty years (and even since the last edition in 2012) that have taken place. So let's look at some of those key changes, challenges, opportunities, and fresh ways God's Spirit is blowing, bringing grace and truth through the church, especially related to these little communities we call small groups.

1. SHIFTS IN THE ROLE OF THE PASTOR

From Sole Leader to Team Leader

In Protestant churches, pastoral leadership has expanded from a single authoritative figure to a team-based, collaborative model. Increasingly, pastors lead alongside associate pastors, ministry directors, and lay leaders (particularly those engaged in group leadership).

Pastor as Vision-Caster and Organizational Leader

Pastors today not only preach and provide pastoral care but also function as organizational developers, vision-casters, and brand storytellers. In large churches, the role of "lead pastor/CEO" has arisen, where a senior pastor leads strategically and the staff members handle operational tasks.

Specialization in Pastoral Roles

There has been an increase in specialized pastors—small group pastors, teaching pastors, executive pastors, worship pastors, family pastors, digital pastors, and community-life pastors. The digital or online pastor has also emerged as churches have expanded their online services and social media outreach—a trend that became especially prevalent after the COVID-19 pandemic accelerated online ministry.

Increasing Number of Women in Leadership Roles

Some churches and denominations, in accord with their theological or ministerial convictions, do not allow women in leadership roles (such as senior pastor or teaching pastor), or as small group leaders when men are in the group, or as elders, or in other senior governance roles. Nonetheless, there has been a growing number of women in the top leadership roles in seminaries, denominations, churches, and various other church and parachurch ministry roles.

2. THE EXPANSION OF A SMALL-GROUPS PHILOSOPHY OF MINISTRY

Small Groups No Longer Seen as Optional

It is often no longer a decision of *whether* a church will have small groups but *how* the church will implement those groups. Today, you might attend a church *with* groups, where you have options—like choosing a Sunday school class. Or you might attend a church *of* groups, where every ministry has groups as part of it—like the small groups in the men's ministry. Or you may attend a church that *is* small groups, where you are expected to be in a group because that is how the church is structured—and is what makes you a member of the church.

Small Groups as a Core Discipleship Model

Since the mid-1990s, small groups have moved from optional programs to central discipleship processes. Group models have become popular in cell churches, megachurches, house churches (where they have experienced a rebirth), micro-churches, and other types of churches that rely on them as the primary way to foster spiritual growth, accountability, and community.

Variation of Groups

Over the decades, various forms and models have emerged. Groups today vary in size, meeting format, and meeting location. Post-COVID 2020, many churches began to incorporate Zoom and asynchronous platforms (e.g., WhatsApp, Facebook, Google Meet) as small group formats. These online groups allow believers to overcome mobility issues, limited access, and irregular schedules that would otherwise impede personal contact. Some groups are formed based on geography and neighborhood connections (urban and suburban), some are formed out of the affinities that people share (pilots, athletes, marketplace workers, etc.), and some are shaped around shared mission or shared provision of care.

Many groups are formed based around practices such as prayer, Bible study, solitude, silence, decision-making, and discernment. Some involve recovery ministries (AA and all the similar anonymous groups), while others provide needed support (grief support, divorce support, and various therapeutic needs). There has also been an emergence of gender-based groups, age-based groups, stage-of-life-based groups, culture-and-race-based groups, and groups based on generational formats (such as Gen X, Y, and Z).

Decentralized Pastoral Care

Small group leaders increasingly find themselves as key caregivers in larger churches with thousands of members, where small group networks provide pastoral support, prayer, and practical care—reducing the burden on pastors and staff.

Multiplication and Volunteer Leadership Development

Small-group models have become frameworks for leadership training, a core pipeline in developing volunteers and future ministry leaders.

3. CHANGES IN CHURCH SIZE AND THE RISE OF MEGACHURCHES

Growth of Megachurches (2,000+ attendees)

Megachurches expanded globally from the 1990s to the 2020s and delivered a variety of features: multiple services, large staffs, targeted ministries, high-tech media, and an array of means to attract attendees who could be connected to small groups of all kinds.

Multi-Site and Multi-Campus Churches

Beginning in the early 2000s, churches began launching multiple campuses instead of just having larger auditoriums. This model allowed expansion without geographical relocation and became one of the dominant growth strategies in evangelical churches—and group life was an essential part.

Emergence of Micro-Churches and House-Church Networks

Meeting in homes or public spaces, these small models are mission-focused, locally targeted, and trend away from large, structured megachurches.

4. CHURCH-PLANTING MOVEMENTS

Denominations and networks such as Acts 29, ARC, Fresh Expressions, and others have gained global influence. Micro-church and missional planting movements prioritize bivocational leadership, minimal funding, neighborhood-level mission, and digital church plants using YouTube and other media. Small groups are essential to many thriving church-planting models.

5. THE RISE OF CHRISTIAN COMMUNITY AS A CENTRAL THEME

Community as the Primary Need

Over the last thirty years, cultural loneliness and social fragmentation have grown, which has inspired many churches to place strong emphasis on "doing life together," belonging, and relational discipleship.

Shift from Program-Driven to Community-Driven Ministry

Churches are increasingly evaluating their success not by attendance or programs but by depth of relationships, participation in small groups, mentoring and discipleship engagement, local service, and communal rhythms.

Community as an Evangelistic Strategy

Many churches today see relational community as the most compelling entry point for seekers, creating spaces where they can "belong before they believe."

Rule of Life, Rhythms, and Spiritual Formation

Many Protestant churches today have rediscovered ancient Christian practices—Sabbath-keeping, contemplative prayer, shared meals, spiritual direction—which foster deeper community and spiritual formation. This reflects a hunger for stability and shared identity in a chaotic world.

SUMMARY

As you can see, the rise of various church growth movements has increased the demand for small groups and trained small-group leaders who can function as key leaders in the church. At the core of this is a call for biblical community where people can gather together and become one in Christ.

BECOMING A BIBLICAL COMMUNITY

THAT THEY MIGHT BE ONE

We are created for community—for oneness—so that we can fully express the beauty, power, and image of God. His central focus is for us, as part of his creation, to become a community that enjoys his presence, demonstrates his love, and serves his purposes in the world—now and forever. The Bible is clear: God never intended for us to be alone.

> The LORD God said, "It is *not good* for the man to be alone. I will make a helper suitable for him."
>
> Now the LORD God had formed out of the ground all the wild animals and all the birds in the sky. He brought them to the man to see what he would name them; and whatever the man called each living creature, that was its name. So the man gave names to all the livestock, the birds in the sky and all the wild animals.
>
> But for Adam *no suitable helper was found*. So the LORD God caused the man to fall into a deep sleep; and while he was sleeping, he took one of the man's ribs and then closed up the place with flesh. Then the LORD God made a woman from the rib he had taken out of the man, and he brought her to the man.
>
> The man said,
>
> "This is now bone of my bones
> and flesh of my flesh;
> she shall be called 'woman,'
> for she was taken out of man."

> That is why a man leaves his father and mother and is united to his wife, and they become one flesh.
>
> Adam and his wife were both naked, and they felt no shame.
>
> — Genesis 2:18–25 (italics added)

From the garden of Eden to the present day, God has always intended for people to be in fellowship—in community—with one another. Adam enjoyed full communion with God as Father, Son, and Spirit. Adam enjoyed a sin-free relationship with God, without the intrusion of pretense, fear, or suspicion to thwart genuine fellowship.

But it was *not good.*

Man had no equal, no partner, no being like him with whom to enjoy mutual fellowship. Adam had relational needs that God and the animals could not satisfy. Adam was greater than creation, something he would rule over and exercise authority over. The triune God was his master and leader, someone whose authority and power far transcended his.

He needed an equal. Not a servant, not a boss, not a slave, not a power broker. Someone like him.

I've heard people say that God is all we need in this life. Well, not according to God. Granted, there are times when all we *have* is God. We are alone, without friends or family to comfort, understand, or support us. In an ideal world—even in a fallen world—God has made it clear that aloneness is never preferred to oneness.

"[The two] become one flesh" (Genesis 2:24).

Though this section of Scripture has clear implications for marriage, marriage is not the essential focus. God does not desire everyone to be married. But he wants his people to become one.

REFLECTION

What Is Oneness?

As you consider your role as a leader of a small group, what ideas come to mind when you think of oneness in your group? What might a small group that experiences oneness look like?

THE TRINITY: THE FIRST SMALL GROUP

It should not surprise us that a shared life in community is the norm. Our triune God—Father, Son, and Holy Spirit—has always dwelled in perfect oneness. Yes, it is a mysterious oneness that we can never fully grasp. But the Bible is clear: Each member of the Trinity is fully divine, and each is totally connected to the other in perfect, relational harmony.

Some have referred to the relationship among members of the Trinity as "the shyness of the Trinity" because of the countercultural nature of their interaction. We must always be careful in describing such mysteries, but for a moment let's indulge the concept, because it does reflect the character of our triune God.

The idea of shyness is used because even though each person is fully God and holds supreme power and authority, there is no haggling over who is greatest, most important, or most deserving of attention. Look at a few statements from the Bible:

- **The Father lifts up the Son.** "This is my Son, whom I have chosen; listen to him" (Luke 9:35). "The Father loves the Son and has placed everything in his hands" (John 3:35).

- **The Son lifts up the Father.** "Don't you believe that I [Jesus] am in the Father, and that the Father is in me? The words I say to you I do not speak on my own authority. Rather, it is the Father, living in me, who is doing his work" (John 14:10).

- **The Son lifts up the Spirit.** "I [Jesus] have much more to say to you, more than you can now bear. But when he, the Spirit of truth, comes, he will guide you into all the truth. He will not speak on his own; he will speak only what he hears, and he will tell you what is yet to come" (John 16:12–13).

- **The Spirit lifts up the Son.** "He [the Spirit] will glorify me [Jesus] because it is from me that he will receive what he will make known to you" (John 16:14).

These are a few examples of how the members of the Trinity—Father, Son, and Spirit—live as one God in three persons without clamoring for attention or competing for glory. God desires us to function in the same way. We are created in his image and are called to reflect the same kind of community that exists in the Trinity. We cannot do it without God's help in this sin-tainted world, but leaning on his power, we strive to reflect that reality.

REFLECTION

The Trinity as "Small Group"

When you think of God as a small group of three persons sharing perfect community, what aspects of that image translate to your group? You are all far from perfect—but is there anything in God's nature that you can emulate in a small group of messed-up human beings?

JESUS: HIS GROUP AND HIS VISION FOR COMMUNITY

When we ponder what it takes to live in oneness, it's clear we are incapable. In fact, most of us don't even know what it would look like to live that way. There are many examples of deep friendship and oneness in the stories of the Bible to guide us, but Jesus of Nazareth stands supreme as our model and guide for community. So let's review some of his practices here on earth and discover his passionate dream for community in the church.

Look at the following sections of the Bible and take a few moments by yourself (or with some other leaders) to jot down some observations from Jesus' prayer for his followers.

A Prayer for Oneness

> "I will remain in the world no longer, but they are still in the world, and I am coming to you. Holy Father, protect them by the power of your name, the name you gave me, so that they may be one as we are one. While I was with them, I protected them and kept them safe by that name you gave me. None has been lost except the one doomed to destruction so that Scripture would be fulfilled.
>
> "I am coming to you now, but I say these things while I am still in the world, so that they may have the full measure of my joy within them. I have given them your word and the world has hated them, for they are not of the world any more than I am of the world. My prayer is not that you take them out of the world but that you protect them from the evil one. They are not of the world, even as I am not of it. Sanctify them by the truth; your word is truth. As you sent me into the world, I have sent them into the world. For them I sanctify myself, that they too may be truly sanctified.

"My prayer is not for them alone. I pray also for those who will believe in me through their message, that all of them may be one, Father, just as you are in me and I am in you. May they also be in us so that the world may believe that you have sent me. I have given them the glory that you gave me, that they may be one as we are one—I in them and you in me—so that they may be brought to complete unity. Then the world will know that you sent me and have loved them even as you have loved me.

"Father, I want those you have given me to be with me where I am, and to see my glory, the glory you have given me because you loved me before the creation of the world.

"Righteous Father, though the world does not know you, I know you, and they know that you have sent me. I have made you known to them, and will continue to make you known in order that the love you have for me may be in them and that I myself may be in them."

— John 17:11–26

You might want to underline a few key phrases or words or simply write them down as you reflect on the questions in the following section.

REFLECTION

Jesus' Prayer for Community

1. As Jesus prays, how often does he repeat his desire that his followers be one? What does this tell you?

2. From your reading of this prayer, why is oneness so important to Jesus? What does he say will be the result of our becoming one?

3. In this section of Jesus' prayer, he lists some of the things he wants us to share with the Trinity. Some he has given us; some he asks the Father to provide. What are they?

Jesus longs for his followers to share in the fellowship of the Trinity—not simply to model it, understand it, or to talk about it—but to *experience* it.

"May they also be in us" (verse 21), he prays. Wow! Jesus desires that we enter into the small group of the Trinity to experience what he experiences in that community. That is profound. So never think of yourself as "just" a small group leader in your church.

You are inviting others to join you in the fellowship of the Trinity!

Jesus and His Group

One of Jesus' first priorities was to form a community of disciples, similar to those of the other rabbis of his day. Unlike the individualized educational approaches in most Western cultures today, communal learning was central to Jewish education. Even though Jesus' disciples were mostly uneducated and not typical rabbinic students, he wanted to be with them. He didn't just teach them; he spent a considerable amount of time in fellowship with them.

> Jesus went up on a mountainside and called to him those he wanted, and they came to him. He appointed twelve that they might be with him and that he might send them out to preach and to have authority to drive out demons. These are the twelve he appointed: Simon (to whom he gave the name Peter), James son of Zebedee and his brother John (to them he gave the name Boanerges, which means "sons of thunder"), Andrew, Philip, Bartholomew, Matthew, Thomas, James son of Alphaeus, Thaddaeus, Simon the Zealot and Judas Iscariot, who betrayed him.
>
> — Mark 3:13–19

However, we can learn much from Jesus' work with his disciples—and certainly declare the priority that communal group life had in his ministry strategy. Following the disciples through the four Gospels, we see they did a lot together: eating, traveling, sleeping, teaching, healing, praying, listening, learning, failing, arguing, and scheming. They did much of life *together* as they observed the Master's interaction with people and sat under his teaching.

Notice, Jesus chose the twelve "that they might be with him" (verse 14) before sending them out into ministry—a ministry that, compared to the group you are leading, likely had some unique qualities. But you can be *with them* as Jesus was with his little community.

The key to becoming a community is being together as frequently as possible: at meals, church services, ministry gatherings, serving opportunities, prayer times, group meetings, those meeting-after-the-meeting moments, and when the group members need extra help or care. This doesn't mean that every group member has to be present and interacting at every gathering. As long as they are connecting throughout the week—by phone, by email, over coffee, chatting after a service—you will see the level of community increase.

Community in the New Testament

Community is a theme that runs throughout Scripture. God has always been calling out a people for himself, beginning with Israel and continuing with the church. Even when the Jews were dispersed among enemy nations during times of captivity, they organized themselves into groups and ultimately formed synagogues (Jewish communities of worship and teaching) where they could serve others and live out their beliefs.

It was natural, therefore, for Jesus to develop a community of followers and for Paul, Peter, and other church planters to start new communities wherever they went as they proclaimed the gospel. These new communities began as small groups, just as Jesus had modeled with the twelve disciples (Mark 3:14; Luke 6:12–19).

Community-focused groups were an integral part of the early church strategy. They were small enough to allow members to minister to one another, use their spiritual gifts, and mature in the teachings of Christ. They were vibrant and life-giving communities where evangelism and service could take place as outsiders watched a loving and compassionate community in action. Small groups created a sense of oneness while also reaching a lost world for Christ. These groups devoted themselves to the teaching of the apostles, to fellowship with one another, to practicing the Lord's Supper together, and to praying for one another. They were characterized by mutuality, accountability, service, love, and evangelism.

Meeting in smaller groups allowed each member to discover and use their spiritual gifts to serve other members in the body. These groups encouraged them and allowed them to build up one another so the body of Christ could be cared for and the world could be influenced through their good deeds.

BECOMING A COMMUNITY, ONE LIFE AT A TIME

If you are like me, you want instant community. Have a few meetings, pray, read, laugh, cry, and *bang*—community! Building community will take some time and effort. But you can count on this: The rewards are worth it. Remember the first time you connected deeply with someone who was on the same mission and seeking the same purposes in God's kingdom? Remember the thrill (but also the work it took) when you came together and worked through the relational snags that go along with every venture into oneness?

I do.

Back in 1982, a group of about sixteen people forever transformed my life. I was in the Philadelphia area after graduating from college and working a year in New York City. My banking job was an exciting new adventure, and I was enjoying the freedom that money and singleness afforded to a twenty-three-year-old male. I had just become a follower of Jesus, but the church setting I was in was not conducive to much spiritual growth.

One evening after a softball game, a friend from high school walked over from an adjacent field, and we quickly got reacquainted. We had played football together but had almost no interaction since those glory days five years earlier.

"Hey, I heard you're a Christian now," he remarked with a smirk.

"Uh . . . yes, kind of a new thing in my life," I said, somewhat sheepishly, not knowing where a conversation like this would go.

My friend smiled broadly. "Me too!" he said. "It happened in college and really changed my life." I remembered feeling relieved at this point, no longer fearing that some kind of persecution was coming my way. (After all, he was carrying a baseball bat.)

"Just heard you were back in town," my friend continued. "There are some others from our high school days who get together in a small group every week at my house. We pray, read the Bible, and have a lot of fun. Would you like to come?"

"Sure," I found myself saying. "Just let me know when and where."

I had no clue at this time what a small group of Jesus people was like. I had no idea that this group would transform my life, my career path, my relationships with women, and my adventure in church leadership. But it did.

- I found real friends there, both men and women. (Before becoming a Christ follower, I hadn't done much to build friendships with women I didn't date.)
- I discovered a deep connection with God and with a few group members who made me feel safe but also accountable.
- I ended an unhealthy relationship with the woman I was dating.
- I left the bank to enter seminary for some ministry training.
- I began to understand how a small group becomes a community that transforms a life—forever.
- I moved from feeling separated from God's people to experiencing the oneness in Christian fellowship—the kind that God himself experiences and enjoys.

As you move through this material, my prayer is that you will find the same experience as a leader and as a participant in a group. Let the adventure begin.

REFLECTION

Your Journey Toward Community

As you think of your own journey into a life-changing community, what comes to mind? Was it smooth and simple? A hard road? Describe some of your reactions and what you have learned from experiences in groups and teams that might help you as you lead your small group.

ADDITIONAL RESOURCES

Dietrich Bonhoeffer, *Life Together* (HarperCollins, 1954). This classic by the persecuted World War II German pastor unpacks the reality and spiritual power of Christian community as we connect with others in Word, prayer, sacrament, and living together in the name of Jesus.

Larry Crabb, *The Safest Place on Earth* (W, 1999). This focuses on the environment that is most conducive to developing spiritual community with others.

Bill Donahue, *The Irresistible Community* (Baker Books, 2015). This focuses on three ways Jesus practiced community life and modeled it for the Twelve—by sharing fellowship at the table, by picking up a towel to serve others, and by living in the fullness of God's truth.

Julie Gorman, *Community That Is Christian* (Baker Books, 2nd ed., 2002). A biblical and practical handbook for building small group ministry and leading effective groups.

Andy Stanley and Bill Willits, *Creating Community* (PHR Christian Publishing, 2021). Teaches how to foster meaningful community, whether face-to-face or online, by creating a small-group culture through a proven five-step strategy.

CHAPTER 1

CLARIFYING YOUR PURPOSE

SPIRITUAL GROWTH AND COMMUNITY: RELATIONAL AND PERSONAL

Committed, authentic relationships have always been an essential component in the process of growth. This truth is a universal principle and not just limited to the Christian life. Sociologists, psychologists, and health care workers agree that people who have strong relationships experience greater peace and joy, heal more quickly, and have fewer emotional health problems than those who live disconnected lives.

Community is at the core of the church and is essential to both evangelism and discipleship. As author and theologian Howard Snyder writes, "At its most basic level the church is a community, not a hierarchy; an organism, not an organization (Matthew 18:20; Romans 12:5–8; 1 Corinthians 12; Ephesians 4:1–16; 1 Peter 4:10–11)."[1]

Later he adds, "Many churches do not share the gospel effectively because their communal experience of the gospel is too weak and tasteless to be worth sharing.... But where Christian fellowship demonstrates the gospel, believers come alive and sinners get curious and want to know what the secret is. So true Christian community (*koinonia*) becomes both the basis and the goal of evangelism.... The community is the only effective school for discipleship. For these reasons, building true *koinonia* is an indispensable link in the life cycle of church growth."[2]

Therefore, if we expect change to occur in people's lives, the community life of the church must be central—the epicenter of both the work of the Spirit and the transformational power of the Word.

The church, of course, has its roots in the Old Testament promises to Abraham, whose family was the first community to live out God's purpose for the world as a blessing to all nations. Later, as Israel came into being through Jacob, families became a central force for growth and life, followed closely by clans and tribes. Communal life flourished through these relational structures, which provided security, support during challenging times, strength in numbers, and the means of training up children in the ways of God. You might say that when God wanted to reach a community, he built one first—calling forth a team, a tribe, or a family—that could reach the world.

"ONE ANOTHERS" OF THE NEW TESTAMENT

A new community in Christ was birthed in Acts 2, and from that time, a communal life not limited to family boundaries took precedence. Even under Jesus' teaching, it was clear that the nuclear family was not equivalent to the family of God, the church: "While Jesus was still talking to the crowd, his mother and brothers stood outside, wanting to speak to him. Someone told him, 'Your mother and brothers are standing outside, wanting to speak to you.' He replied to him, 'Who is my mother, and who are my brothers?' Pointing to his disciples, he said, 'Here are my mother and my brothers. For whoever does the will of my Father in heaven is my brother and sister and mother'" (Matthew 12:46–50).

This new emphasis on the church, and not the nuclear family or tribe, as the primary expression of community is scattered throughout the pages of the New Testament. A number of statements imply, if they do not directly teach, that it's in relationships—in groups, families, mission teams, friendships, and so on—that the faith is learned, practiced, and witnessed by the world. Here are some of the most common examples:

- Be at peace with one another (Mark 9:50).
- Love one another (John 13:34).
- Be devoted to one another (Romans 12:10).
- Honor one another (Romans 12:10).
- Live in harmony with one another (Romans 12:16).
- Stop passing judgment on one another (Romans 14:13).
- Accept one another (Romans 15:7).
- Instruct one another (Romans 15:14).
- Greet one another (Romans 16:16).
- Serve one another (Galatians 5:13).
- Carry one another's burdens (Galatians 6:2).
- Be patient and bear with one another in love (Ephesians 4:2).
- Be kind and compassionate to one another (Ephesians 4:32).
- Forgive one another (Ephesians 4:32).
- Speak to one another with psalms, hymns, and spiritual songs (Ephesians 5:19).
- Submit to one another out of reverence for Christ (Ephesians 5:21).
- In humility consider one another better than yourself (Philippians 2:3).
- Teach one another (Colossians 3:16).
- Admonish one another (Colossians 3:16).
- Encourage one another (1 Thessalonians 4:18).
- Build up one another (1 Thessalonians 5:11).
- Spur one another on toward love and good deeds (Hebrews 10:24).
- Do not slander one another (James 4:11).

- Don't grumble against one another (James 5:9).
- Confess your sins to one another (James 5:16).
- Pray for one another (James 5:16).
- Clothe yourselves with humility toward one another (1 Peter 5:5).

Imagine your group fleshing out these "one anothers" as you live the way of Jesus. Imagine what would happen around you. Imagine how families and workplaces would be different, how neighborhoods and schools would be transformed, and how skeptics and critics might have their hearts opened to the gospel.

Just imagine!

REFLECTION

Relational Discipleship

Take a few moments to ponder the connection between spiritual growth in Christ and our need for relationships. If you or your group got serious about this biblical idea, what might the future look like for all of you? How might this change the way you understand and pursue discipleship?

Since relationships help the body grow toward maturity in Christ (Ephesians 4:16), your group's mission must focus on making disciples in the context of community. Whether your group is made up of spiritual seekers, newer followers of Christ, or lifelong Christians, consider your mission to be the spiritual formation of disciples.

WHAT IS A DISCIPLE (FOLLOWER) OF JESUS?

Before crafting a mission statement, it's good to discuss what it means to be a disciple of Christ. The Bible gives us no clear definition of a disciple in a single verse or paragraph. Much of the Bible, of course, describes what the life of a follower of Jesus looks like. Many churches and parachurch organizations have tried to define *discipleship* or *disciple* so that people in their churches or ministries are clear about their goal. Such definitions can be helpful, as long as it is made clear they are only attempts to create a general description, not an exhaustive definition, of the characteristics of a follower of Jesus.

In the Bible, we find that disciples came in all shapes and sizes. They had different backgrounds, gifts, experiences, and levels of spiritual maturity. Some gave their lives for Christ, but some failed under pressure. Some followed only for a while to get their needs met and then left when Jesus' teaching or call to commitment got too intense (John 6:60–71).

Your church or ministry's description of a disciple needs to be a good framework on which to build a way of life in the kingdom of God, so be cautious when you define what a disciple is. Definitions can easily be used to judge people or to wrongly deny someone opportunities for leadership or development. Strive instead to describe the heart, beliefs, attitudes, and activities of followers of Jesus to which we can all aspire as we "spur one another on toward love and good deeds" (Hebrews 10:24).

The focus of making disciples of Jesus should be on the "of Jesus" part. The focus is not on our systems, definitions, processes, and measurements—as helpful and necessary as those things may be. Rather, the focus is on observing Jesus' character, mission, and life, and on encouraging one another to trust and follow him fully. "The student is not above the teacher, nor a servant above his master. It is enough for students to be *like their teachers*, and servants *like their masters*" (Matthew 10:24–25, emphasis added).

We are called to be like Jesus. Never lose sight of that goal. A disciple is a follower of Jesus Christ who seeks to obey his teachings and to imitate his way of life.

As much as possible, make sure your description aligns with the description provided by the leadership of your church or ministry. To the degree that you can adapt that description to your group, do so. Work with your leadership to ensure your group is aligned with your church or ministry.

Take some time to jot down some characteristics—beliefs, actions, character—of a follower of Jesus. Don't worry about naming every possible trait and commitment (that would cover most of the New Testament!). Instead, just write down a few core concepts, or simply copy your church's description if one exists.

REFLECTION

Description of a Disciple

A follower or disciple of Jesus is:

Now that you have an idea of what a disciple is, let's look at your group's mission to work together as a community to become more fully devoted followers of Jesus.

MISSION

What are we doing together?

A clear mission is key to your group's success. Every mission has a few key components. The larger and more complex the group, the more detailed the mission needs to be so that everyone understands it. Every group needs focus, but not every group needs as much detail.

On pages 7–8 is an exercise to work through as you develop your group's mission. It's fine if you cannot complete all of it now. You might want to work through this exercise as a group, gaining clarity and consensus as you move along. Depending on the nature and focus of your group, you may even decide to skip parts of it.

Crafting Your Mission Statement

The goal is not to take everything you just wrote in the sidebar and cram it into a mission statement. Instead, use what you have written to clarify what your focus will be. Not every group can be everything for everyone.

The key questions are: *What is our unique mission as a group? Who are we and what are we going to try to do together for the next few months?* You can revise the mission statement every six months or so, depending on the needs and direction of your group.

The following three steps can help you create your mission statement.

Step 1

First, "determine your infinitive." An infinitive is a phrase that begins with the word *to.* The phrase you write may depend on what kind of group you are leading. (If you are not sure what kind of group you want to lead, see appendix 1, "Common Categories of Small Groups," for ideas.) Some examples of infinitives include:

- To become
- To learn
- To experience
- To empower
- To practice
- To create
- To build
- To serve
- To discover

DEVELOPING YOUR GROUP MISSION

1. What characteristics do we expect of disciples in our group? (Note that the purpose of this exercise is to gain perspective and set some goals for development, not to compile a legalistic checklist.)

   Beliefs:

   Attitudes:

   Commitments:

   Spiritual Practices:

   Actions and Service:

continued on the next page

2. How will our group help the disciple-making process?

   Format of Meetings:

   Use of the Bible:

   Use of Discussion Materials:

   Role of Prayer:

   Environment to Create (safety, respect, honor, and so on):

   Activities or Other Gatherings:

Step 2

Next, write a "by means of" or "through" phrase that defines your process or approach to the mission. For example, "through Bible study and prayer" or "by practicing an authentic faith."

Step 3

Finally, write a "so that" or "in order to" phrase. For example, a women's group might write: "In order to become Christ-centered mothers who can guide younger moms through the difficult months following childbirth." A group whose approach to its mission is through learning the core doctrines of the Christian faith might write: "So that we can discern truth from error and build confidence in our beliefs."

Sample Mission Statements

- "To create an environment characterized by grace, truth, and humility so that our nonbelieving friends will discover the group as a safe place to share their lives and observe authentic Christlike love and relationships."
- "To challenge and support one another toward full devotion to Christ by providing an environment for connection with God, authentic community, and spiritual formation."
- "To make disciples of Jesus Christ by equipping one another through engagement with Scripture, mutual accountability, holy living, and sacrificial service to others so that our families and communities will see Jesus' love in action."

REFLECTION

Writing Your Mission Statement

Take a few moments to craft your mission statement using these three steps.

To:

continued on the next page

By or through:

So that:

VALUES

Why are we gathering as a group? What do we believe about the environment we are creating in which to grow together?

Values are your underlying beliefs about your small group. They are not doctrinal beliefs but rather the firmly held principles that govern how you will function together, treat one another, and create an environment conducive to accomplishing your mission.

For example, an organization trains people to be effective classroom teachers because they hold a value: Every student deserves a quality teacher. A recovery group uses the twelve-steps strategy because they hold a value: People need a safe, authentic community to provide the support essential to overcoming addictive behavior.

Most small groups have a set of fundamental values about group life. Here are a few:

- **Safety:** Creating a place free of judgment and condemnation in order to build a foundation for trust.
- **Authenticity:** Being real about pain, struggles, joys, hopes, dreams, fears, thoughts, and feelings. Avoiding pretense and putting on a false self to hide real issues and needs.
- **Care:** Expressing concern and support to one another with words and actions.
- **Growth:** Having a desire for the group members to make progress in life—spiritually, emotionally, and relationally.

- **Confidentiality:** Promising not to talk to people outside the group about what people share and do in the group.
- **Respect:** Honoring each person's right to have opinions and recognizing their dignity as human beings.

Later in this book, you will be guided through the process of setting ground rules—or "covenants," as some groups call them. This process includes naming and clarifying your core values.

For now, it is important that you begin thinking about values in light of your group's mission or purpose. As a leader, it is sometimes essential (or even expected) that you lead your group through the process of discussing its values together by having some ideas of your own. Starting with a blank slate and asking, "So what do you think our values should be?" is too open-ended an approach for most people.

REFLECTION

Writing Your Values List

Take a few moments to list five or six core values of your group. Then define each one and prioritize them by placing numbers next to them. Remember, you will process these later with your group.

-
-
-
-
-
-

VISION

Where are we going together? What will it look like when we arrive?

If the mission (*What are we doing?*) is the itinerary for a trip, the vision (*What does the destination look like?*) is the travel brochure.

One time, my wife and I traveled to Italy for a speaking engagement. I was excited to go there because of the brochure I had seen, not the itinerary. The photographs of the majestic artwork and ancient ruins of Rome, Florence, and Capri—and of the romantic countryside surrounding those cities—created in me a desire to go to Italy. The itinerary—departure times, airline seats, hotel locations, travel dates, time spent in each city—was crucial to the success of the trip, but there was little there to inspire me.

When people asked, "Where are you going in Italy?" we didn't answer, "We're flying to Rome on a Boeing 757. We'll be sitting in seats 23A and 23B for eight hours and forty-two minutes, then land on a runway, and then get our bags, and then . . ." No, we said, "After a few days in Rome at the Coliseum and seeing all the ancient sites, we're headed to Florence for a beautiful lunch on the veranda of a villa overlooking a vineyard! Then we're going to see Michelangelo's *David* at the Academia Gallery . . ."

Vision inspires and motivates. It provides a picture of a preferred future—something you are moving toward together and want to become as you accomplish the mission.

Completing a mission solves a problem; pursuing a vision fulfills a longing. One moves the hands; the other stirs the heart.

For example, your group might be studying a parenting curriculum to learn biblical principles for raising your kids, but that is not the vision. That is the *mission*. The vision might be, "To become caring, godly parents who raise our children with tender discipline, bold love, and creative, fun-filled engagement."

Vision Questions

Before you work through the following questions, *note that chapter 5 of this book presents material that is to be used* by the whole group. *But at this time, you will be thinking only about your vision and will be working alone on the material in the following section. When you meet with your group, you will use this material and the information in chapter 5 to help the entire group embrace a vision. If you are just training for leadership at the moment and are not actively leading a group, the following material will help you get started.*

Here are a few questions to prompt the development of your vision. Keep in mind your group's mission and values as you take a few minutes to dream about the future. What might it be like when God works through and in your group to accomplish your mission?

1. What do we want to become? What kind of group?
2. What will our lives look like if we complete the mission?
3. How will our relationships feel?
4. What kind of community will we experience?
5. How will others be different if we reach them with our mission?
6. How will the culture or workplace or neighborhood look when we are successful?
7. How might our families or marriages or dating relationships feel?

Vision statements are generally shorter than mission statements. Your vision statement might be something like "To be a place where no one stands alone" or "To become fully devoted fathers with passion for our kids" or "To create a neighborhood where the love of Jesus impacts every family's story."

REFLECTION

Writing Your Vision Statement

Write your vision statement here:

PUTTING IT ALL TOGETHER

Now that you have drafted your mission statement, values list, and vision statement, use the following sidebar to summarize your work so you can easily refer to it in the months and years ahead.

THE PURPOSE OF OUR GROUP: CLARITY AND GROWTH

Our Mission:

Our Values:

Our Vision:

ADDITIONAL RESOURCES

George Barna, *The Power of Vision* (Baker Books, 2018). The fact this resource is in its third edition testifies to its impact and usefulness for shaping and communicating vision.

Bill Donahue and Russ Robinson, *Building a Life-Changing Small Group Ministry* (Zondervan, 2012). The early sections of this book describe the philosophy and theology of group life and making disciples.

Will Mancini, *Church Unique* (Jossey-Bass, 2008). This resource helps churches think creatively about their unique vision. Mancini's "Vision Frame" is a great approach to shaping vision.

Greg Ogden, *Discipleship Essentials* (InterVarsity, 2007). This book provides a clear, structured process for guiding a cluster of people along a discipleship journey.

Andy Stanley, *Visioneering* (Multnomah, 2005). Stanley draws on the story of Nehemiah in the Bible to reveal how we can identify and frame a personal vision for living our lives in Christ.

Notes

1. Howard A. Snyder, *The Community of the King* (InterVarsity Press, 1977), 73.
2. Snyder, *The Community of the King*, 147.

CHAPTER 2

FORGING YOUR LEADERSHIP

WHAT KIND OF LEADER DO YOU NEED TO BECOME?

People often say, "Leadership is the whole ball game." We know from Scripture and experience that ministry will not be sustained for long without God-inspired leaders to rally people to the cause and encourage them along the way. Look at any of the biblical leaders—Abraham, Deborah, David, Peter, Paul, Phoebe, Lydia, and the rest—and you will see that God works through men and women to shepherd and mobilize his people. This is not to elevate leaders unnecessarily, because leaders, first and foremost, are servants.

Small groups thrive with qualified leaders. In this chapter, I want to help you understand the incredible privileges—and responsibilities—associated with leadership. I want you to gain clarity about what a small group leader is, what the leader's ministry looks like, and how to do some self-leadership that will keep you growing and effective. It's a good thing to aspire to leadership, but you must always do a quick heart check. So, as you consider the kind of leader you need to become, let's check your motivation for leading others.

BIBLICAL FOUNDATIONS: FOUR KEY PRINCIPLES

1. Leaders Are Christ-Centered

Every believer needs to connect daily with Christ, but this is especially true for group leaders. From Christ you draw strength, hope, confidence, and cleansing. You will lead best from an inner life that is growing and developing intimacy with Christ and, in so doing, will call your group toward the same commitment. As Paul said, "Follow my example, as I follow the example of Christ" (1 Corinthians 11:1). It is important in this regard to spend time in God's presence and fill your deep longings for him when you suffer or experience brokenness (Psalm 42:1).

We should seek God's presence in our grief, weakness, sadness, and fear. We know God is seeking us and drawing near to the brokenhearted (Psalm 34:18). Group members can see us authentically seeking God in listening, prayer, inviting his presence, and being real about our need for God's tender mercy in our deepest sorrow. We can all draw strength from one another but often, when friends or family are far, we draw closer to the God who loves us.

Christ-centered leaders become Christlike leaders. This begins with paying attention to the heart—to integrity and character. Proverbs 4:23 exhorts the wise person to "watch over [their] heart with all diligence, for from it flow the springs of life" (NASB). In Matthew 12:35, Jesus—challenging the heart of the Pharisees—says, "The good man brings good things out of the good stored up in him, and the evil man brings evil things out of the evil stored up in him."

People need to be able to trust their leader in the same way they trust Christ. Leadership is *impossible* apart from trust. Leaders who are truthful and trustworthy will contribute to building their character, while those who break trust with people will find it difficult to restore. Paul encouraged Timothy, a young leader, to "set an example for the believers in speech, in conduct, in love, in faith and in purity" (1 Timothy 4:12). Leaders must maintain their integrity and model the Christian life for the rest of the church.

Like Christ, leaders will be tempted. So, as a leader, you must work to protect your heart from thoughts, actions, and attitudes that will corrupt or harden it. You can do this by engaging in self-examination and peer examination, asking people where you have character weaknesses and strengths, and evaluating your own heart before God and with Scripture.

2. Leaders Are Servants

In Scripture, ministry and service are synonymous with leadership. The person who is not willing to serve is not fit to lead. Jesus set the standard when he said, "Even the Son of Man did not come to be served, but to serve, and to give his life as a ransom for many" (Mark 10:45).

Leadership—even Christian leadership—is often patterned after business or political models, which emphasize the organizational component of leadership. The biblical pattern presents a different perspective. Leaders are referred to as shepherds who guide and serve the flock (1 Peter 5:1–3), caring for and developing those around them. Leaders pick up the servant's towel (John 13:1–17) and model the life and leadership of Christ.

Jesus said, "Whoever serves me must follow me; and where I am, my servant also will be. My Father will honor the one who serves me" (John 12:26).

3. Leaders Are Shepherds

You may have the spiritual gift of leadership, or you may be gifted to teach, or you may have mercy gifts, discernment gifts, or other types of giftings. Regardless of your gift mix, you—and all other small group leaders—function as a shepherd. Jesus himself said that he was "the good shepherd" (John 10:11), meaning one who is concerned about the health of the flock.

The term *shepherd* is not familiar today in most Western cultures. *Leader* or *guide* are more common labels. Jesus used the term to describe a certain breed of leadership—a certain role he wanted his leaders to follow. There were other leaders in his day—in government, education, religious and social life—but he chose a rather lowly (and smelly) animal to describe his own leadership style and of those who were to guide the people in his church.

Jesus characterized his ministry in this way: "I am the good shepherd; I know my sheep and my sheep know me" (verse 14). He was willing to lay down his life for the sake of the cause, for the love of the community (verse 15). What does that look like in small-group terms? You will find resources and information in chapter 8 to help you answer that question and that will show you how to create an environment of mutual care in your group.

4. Leaders Work Together

No one leads alone! That has been a mantra of mine for many years. Jesus called his followers into a community to develop them as leaders. When it was time for them to participate in ministry, he sent them out in groups (the twelve apostles in Matthew 10) and in pairs (the seventy-two emerging leaders in Luke 10:1). When needs arose in the early community, teams were appointed to provide gift-based servant leadership (Acts 6).

At virtually every point in the church's development, the leadership structure included a plurality of leaders. Paul appointed elders to lead a church once it was established in any city, and he often worked with one or more partners in his ministry efforts, including men and women in his leadership circle (Romans 16).

As a small group leader, you should model this kind of leadership by working with one or more apprentices or fellow leaders, serving together in community. By doing so, you will share leadership and avoid the temptation to become the only one with a leadership role. Apprenticing will be discussed fully in chapter 4.

AUTHENTIC MOTIVES FOR LEADERSHIP

To Serve Christ

"Whatever you do, work at it with all your heart, as working for the Lord, not for human masters, since you know that you will receive an inheritance from the Lord as a reward. It is the Lord Christ you are serving" (Colossians 3:23–24).

To Bear Fruit in Your Life

"This is to my Father's glory, that you bear much fruit, showing yourselves to be my disciples" (John 15:8).

To Keep Watch Over (Shepherd) Others

"Keep watch over yourselves and all the flock of which the Holy Spirit has made you overseers. Be shepherds of the church of God, which he bought with his own blood" (Acts 20:28).

To Be an Example to the Church

"Be shepherds of God's flock that is under your care, watching over them—not because you must, but because you are willing, as God wants you to be; not pursuing dishonest gain, but eager to serve; not lording it over those entrusted to you, but being examples to the flock. And when the Chief Shepherd appears, you will receive the crown of glory that will never fade away" (1 Peter 5:2–4).

To Use Your Gifts to Serve Others

"So Christ himself gave the apostles, the prophets, the evangelists, the pastors and teachers, to equip his people for works of service, so that the body of Christ may be built up until we all reach unity in the faith and in the knowledge of the Son of God and become mature, attaining to the whole measure of the fullness of Christ" (Ephesians 4:11–13).

To Communicate the Message of Reconciliation

"God was reconciling the world to himself in Christ, not counting people's sins against them. And he has committed to us the message of reconciliation. We are therefore Christ's ambassadors, as though God were making his appeal through us. We implore you on Christ's behalf: Be reconciled to God. God made him who had no sin to be sin for us, so that in him we might become the righteousness of God" (2 Corinthians 5:19–21).

WRONG MOTIVES FOR LEADERSHIP

For Self-Promotion

"Let someone else praise you, and not your own mouth; an outsider, and not your own lips" (Proverbs 27:2).

To Feel Important or Gain Prestige

"We speak as those approved by God to be entrusted with the gospel. We are not trying to please people but God, who tests our hearts. You know we never used flattery, nor did we put on a mask to cover up greed—God is our witness. We were not looking for praise from people, not from you or anyone else" (1 Thessalonians 2:4–6).

Because of Pressure from Others

"Be shepherds of God's flock that is under your care, watching over them—not because you must, but because you are willing, as God wants you to be" (1 Peter 5:2).

HINDRANCES TO LEADERSHIP

Having a Short Fuse or Exhibiting Outbursts of Anger

James tells us that human anger does not achieve the righteousness of God (James 1:19–20). God's work is accomplished by one who listens attentively, speaks only when necessary, and is slow to anger. Leaders put aside anger, manage it properly, and channel it appropriately (Galatians 5:20; Ephesians 4:31; Colossians 3:8).

Unconfessed Sin

We are commanded to confess our sins. John says, "If we confess our sins, he is faithful and just and will forgive us our sins and purify us from all unrighteousness" (1 John 1:9). Any sin that has control of us (Romans 6:16) must be confessed and brought under the lordship of Christ (Acts 2:38). Outstanding sin that is not dealt with appropriately could disqualify a leader.

Biblical Error or False Teaching

Paul warned Timothy to watch for false teachers who lead people away from the faith: "For the time will come when people will not put up with sound doctrine. Instead, to suit their own desires, they will gather around them a great number of teachers to say what their itching ears want to hear. They will turn their ears away from the truth and turn aside to myths" (2 Timothy 4:3–4). Small group leaders study Scripture in order to "correctly [handle] the word of truth" (2 Timothy 2:15) and guide people into a proper understanding of what it says. They do not impose their opinions on a biblical text but seek only to reveal God's truth.

BASIC QUALIFICATIONS FOR SMALL GROUP LEADERSHIP

Who is fit to lead a small group? It's likely your church already has guidelines to answer that question. It's also likely you already meet those guidelines, or are on your way to meeting them, because you are reading this book and working through this material.

There are usually two approaches when it comes to determining who is qualified. Which approach is taken generally depends on a person's view of what a small group should be. Those who view the small group as an all-encompassing disciple-making machine want it to be led by someone like the apostle Paul or Priscilla (another leader in the early church). In these people's view, groups must study the Bible, train members for the entire Christian life, challenge them to missionary service, and cover every category of Christian theology.

On the other extreme are those who think anyone who has a pulse and can fog a mirror could lead a group. Wisdom dictates that we must somehow communicate the significance and seriousness of guiding people toward growth in Christ while also realizing that even gifted leaders need time to acquire all the skills and discernment for effective leading.

Four Core Qualifications

There are four core qualifications you should consider when taking on the leadership challenge or when developing potential leaders. These qualifications are essential for fulfilling a biblical role of leadership. Again, I emphasize that your church will likely bring much clarity to this, so please consider the material to follow as recommendations. Take the time to discuss this with your church leadership in order to align with the mission and purposes of your church.

1. You recognize the Bible as the true Word of God and as authoritative in your life.

Scripture is essential for living life in Christ and in his community, the church. It has authority because it represents the teachings and stories of the triune God through the ages. God is our ultimate authority, and we submit to him. We obey his Word because it comes from him, was given to us by him through his Spirit, and has the power to transform lives.

2. You are in a personal, growing relationship with Jesus Christ, your Savior and Lord.

A leader in the body of Christ is a member of that body. The only way to be a member of the body of Christ is to trust Christ for salvation and for ongoing discipleship—to believe that he has forgiven our sins and calls us to love him and continually obey his teaching. By his grace, and with the help of his Spirit, his Word, and wisdom from others in the body of Christ, we seek to grow toward maturity. A leader is not expected to be *perfect* but is expected to be an active *participant* in pursuit of the kind of life that Jesus has called us toward.

3. You agree to submit to and be accountable to the leaders of your church, whom God has placed in roles of responsibility and authority in his church.

It is a general principle from the Bible that we are to honor, respect, and follow people in authority over us, particularly in the church (Romans 13:1; Hebrews 13:17; 1 Peter 2:13; Titus 3:1). This is not intended to convey some blind allegiance to human authority nor to assume that every leader is worthy of the respect and honor due him or her.

Men and women with leadership gifts have been given roles by God—as apostles, prophets, evangelists, pastors, and teachers (Ephesians 4:11)—to build up the body of Christ. Some of these people, along with those with other kinds of gifts, have been chosen for leadership positions in the church—roles such as elders, deacons, and board or council members (each church uses different terminology).

These leaders are responsible to shepherd God's people toward maturity, to protect the church, and to fulfill God's call for that church to expand God's kingdom on earth.

4. You have the emotional capacity and discernment to guide others in a group process. This implies a potential leader is willing to make the time to guide the group and reserve some energy for that task. The capacity to lead will be compromised if there are great stresses on the person (such as relational breakdown in marriage or family, addictions and sin patterns that are not being addressed, exhaustion, or too many other life commitments).

In addition, there is a level of relational discernment that requires some emotional intelligence. Leaders must have the capacity to relate to people in healthy and productive ways and to discern when and how to engage with others (provide care, show love, express concern, confront destructive attitudes, and so on) as the situation requires.

A leader is *not* a professional counselor or relationship expert—just someone who has a healthy understanding of relationships and has a general awareness of how to deal with the group with grace and truth.

Summary on Basic Qualifications

To sum up, if you: (1) Do not believe the Bible; (2) do not have a growing relationship with Jesus; (3) cannot or will not be accountable to reasonable, godly leaders in the church; and/or (4) cannot bring relational discernment and energy to a leadership role, then you should hit the pause button for becoming a leader at this point in time. Work with your church to determine areas for growth and development that will help you qualify in the future. Your personal growth and relationship to Jesus and his church are more important than your filling a leadership role!

In addition to these qualifications, your church or ministry may have other expectations. For example, some churches will require you to have been a believer for at least one year, or to have been in a small group for a period of time, or to attend classes or training, or to become a church member. These types of reasonable qualifications vary from church to church.

REFLECTION

Leadership Self-Check

1. Am I willing to shape my leadership around the four principles of biblical leadership?

I will be Christ-centered.	Y N
I will view myself as a shepherd.	Y N
I will maintain the posture of a servant.	Y N
I will share leadership with others.	Y N

2. Do I possess the four core qualifications for leadership as outlined in this chapter and as described by the leaders of my church? If not, am I willing to grow in the areas they recommend so that I can someday take on a leadership role? Y N

FOUR CORE LEADERSHIP PRACTICES

In every profession, area of expertise, or skill, there are core practices that are essential to achieving a level of competence and success. A young baseball player must learn to throw, catch, hit, and run the bases. An emerging violinist must learn finger positions, practice scales, understand musical terminology, and have an ear for tone and pitch. Bankers must become experts at attracting new customers, making quality loans, and managing cash effectively. What, then, are the core practices of a group leader? Every effective and transformational small group leader does five things—*listen, learn, love, lead,* and *look.*

1. Listen

I once asked a church leader and trained Christian psychologist what he would teach a room filled with small group leaders if he had them for an entire day. He wasted no time answering.

"I would train them to listen!" he said with great conviction.

"And what about the rest of the day?" I asked.

"That's it," he replied, speaking to me as if I were a small child who had just asked how to build a nuclear submarine. "We'd spend *the whole day* on listening."

The whole day? Now I was listening!

Listening is essential in any relationship, especially in marriages and families. Small groups, in particular, must navigate a more complex relational environment because of the sheer numbers of people involved (often six to fifteen). A leader must practice the art of active listening so that they can fully engage with God and with the group members.

The Bible affirms that listening—*really listening*—is the mark of a wise person:

> He who answers before listening—that is his folly and his shame (Proverbs 18:13).
>
> Even fools are thought wise if they keep silent, and discerning if they hold their tongues (Proverbs 17:28).

Listening doesn't simply mean not talking, though that can help if you tend to interrupt and live in the world of Proverbs 18:13. Active listening means asking questions, making observations, feeding back information to the speaker, and seeking greater understanding of what is being discussed. Active listening involves not only what you *hear* but also what you *say*.

This means engaging with the speaker, setting aside your personal agenda, and keeping yourself from distracting thoughts (particularly about what you're going to say next!). Here are some tips for active listening.

What You Say

1. Invite comments from the group.
2. Empathize with people's emotions.
3. Explore their statements, seeking more information.
4. Clarify what has been said.

What You Hear

1. *Verbal* (the content of what is said). Sometimes you may be so interested in what you are about to say that you fail to hear the simple facts in a discussion. As you listen, focus on people's names, events, dates, and other specific information being shared.
2. *Nonverbal* (how the content is expressed). Listen for congruity; that is, whether the nonverbal messages match the verbal messages. Do this in three areas:

    - *Facial expressions.* When someone says, "I'm okay," does their facial expression actually communicate, "I'm a little sad"?

- *Tone of voice.* Listen for tones of sarcasm, anger, sadness, enthusiasm, hesitancy, fear, and so on.
- ***Body movements and posture.*** Are arms and legs crossed and closed? Are people fidgety or relaxed? Does their posture indicate interest or boredom? Remember, you can "hear" a lot just by watching people's actions.

The following table compares active listening with a passive form of listening that is not really engaged. As a leader, consider how you would rate yourself on each point.

Listening Skills

Passive Versus Active Listening

	Passive Listening	**Active Listening**
Attitude	Rejecting, critical. *"I'm really not interested."*	Receptive, accepting. *"I really want to hear."*
Focus	Me—what I want to say. *"What do I think?"*	Other person—what that person is saying. *"What does he mean?"*
Response	Express what I've been thinking. *"I think you should . . ."*	Clarify first what I've heard the other person say. *"You think . . ." "Do you feel . . ."*
Message	What the person said isn't important. *"I didn't really hear what you said."*	I heard both the feeling and the need in the message. *"I heard what you said."*
Results	Speaker experiences frustration, anger. *Listener communicates, "I don't care."*	Speaker is willing to compromise or tell more. *Listener says, "I care about what you said."*

(Note that this would be great material to review with your group, especially if it's just starting.)

Favorite Phrases Used by Active Listeners

- "Please tell me more about that."
- "Let me see if I understood what you just said."
- "Could you repeat that last idea? I really want to hear that clearly."
- "As you said those words, it sounded as though you might be [happy, sad, angry, excited, tender, confused, scared, reluctant, and so on], and I wanted to see if that is accurate."
- "As you described that situation, I could not help but feel [describe what you felt], and I wondered if you felt the same way."

- "That must have been [hard, easy, exciting, awkward, challenging, painful, and so on] for you."
- "Am I understanding you correctly?"
- "Is there anything you were hoping I would understand, feel, or decide as a result of our conversation?"

The Impact of Really Listening

- Others feel and believe you really care.
- Others respect you.
- Others view you as safe and a person in whom they can confide.
- Others learn to listen as they watch and hear you.
- You earn the right to lead people to new areas of growth.
- You are able to confront difficult people and situations with grace and skill.
- You really learn about people—their thoughts, emotions, needs, concerns, hopes.
- You gain insight for how and where to guide a discussion.
- You discover how to express care and love to others.
- You help seekers and skeptics open up and express contrary points of view.
- Trust grows.
- Relationships deepen.
- People bring hidden parts of life to the surface.

By listening well, you build a foundation for the remaining core practices of a group leader.

REFLECTION

Improving My Listening

I need to grow in my ability to be an active listener by:

2. Learn

Jesus wanted every follower—and particularly every leader—to be a learner. At the end of his most decisive and provocative teaching, the Sermon on the Mount, he makes these challenging comments: "Everyone who hears these words of mine and puts them into practice is like a wise man who built his house on the rock. The rain came down, the streams rose, and the winds blew and beat against that house; yet it did not fall, because it had its foundation on the rock. But everyone who hears these words of mine and does not put them into practice is like a foolish man who built his house on sand. The rain came down, the streams rose, and the winds blew and beat against that house, and it fell with a great crash" (Matthew 7:24–27).

Someone has said, "When you are through learning, you're through!" This is so true! Leaders are learners—and learning will help you maintain your leadership edge.

Paul wanted Timothy to work at his teaching so that he would be a competent communicator of God's truth. He said, "Do your best to present yourself to God as one approved, a worker who does not need to be ashamed and who correctly handles the word of truth" (2 Timothy 2:15). Being good at your ministry really counts.

Becoming competent means pursuing personal development and skill training for the ministry in which you serve. Basic small group skills are necessary regardless of the kind of group you lead, but many types of groups require specific training as well. Identify your core abilities and then work hard to sharpen those competencies while acquiring additional leadership skills.

People know that leaders are far from perfect. They sin, make mistakes, and have flaws that all humans share. However, people do expect their leaders to be in the game and growing in their character, skills, and knowledge. Consider David in the Bible. At times he failed, struggled, and labored to lead God's people—his flock—with integrity and with skill. We all know he wasn't perfect. Yet he was in the game. "David shepherded them with integrity of heart; with skillful hands he led them" (Psalm 78:72). David's life and leadership were characterized by faith, a heart for God, and a willingness to repent and grow.

David was also a learner. Look at Psalm 78 again, a few verses earlier: "[God] chose David his servant and took him from the sheep pens; from tending the sheep he brought him to be the shepherd of his people Jacob, of Israel his inheritance" (verses 70–71). God used David's skill and experience from other aspects of his life for spiritual leadership in Israel.

So what have you learned so far about leading? About group life? What skills do you possess and what skills do you need to master? Take a few moments to complete the following checklist to see where you might need additional growth or training.

Skill Assessment	**I Need Development**	**I Am Strong**
Vision casting	☐	☐
Raising up an apprentice leader	☐	☐
Modeling accountability	☐	☐
Planning a meeting	☐	☐
Asking good questions	☐	☐
Leading discussions	☐	☐
Using the Bible in groups	☐	☐
Choosing curriculum	☐	☐
Opening a meeting creatively	☐	☐
Using a variety of prayers in groups	☐	☐
Evaluating progress	☐	☐
Providing care between meetings	☐	☐
Building relationships	☐	☐
Praying for members	☐	☐
Resolving conflict	☐	☐
Meeting special needs	☐	☐
Serving with others	☐	☐
Practicing listening skills	☐	☐
Promoting growth	☐	☐
Adding new members	☐	☐
Breaking into subgroups for prayer and discussion	☐	☐

In addition to your own assessment of your skills, ask the people who recruited you as a leader, or ask some trusted friends or ministry partners, to assess you on the same topics. Consider asking members of the group you were in before you became a leader. Peer evaluation and honest feedback will help you design a growth strategy for your leadership.

Determine to learn about your group members—about their lives, families, passions, gifts, dreams, and so on. It will help you pray for them and serve them. Regularly attending church services and classes will also help you learn about the Bible and the core doctrines of the faith so that you can lead with increasing confidence and wisdom. Contact your pastor or ministry leader for recommendations (a Study Bible and/or single-volume commentary is a good place to start) and check your church's library (if you have one) for other resources.

As you become a learner—in every area—you will discover more about God and your group. You'll also learn about yourself, especially about your gifts and where best to use them. For instance, perhaps you are feeling frustrated in your current leadership role. It could be you are in the wrong ministry (working with kids, for example, instead of adults). In 1 Corinthians 12:4–7, it is clear that each Christ follower has a gift (or has gifts) for building up the body of Christ. Your gifts—combined with your unique God-given abilities, personality, and experiences—will flourish in some ministry areas and be stunted in others. So it's important to know the kind of small group ministry that best aligns with how God made you.

Take time to assess whether you would fit best with adults or children, working at a task or providing care to the hurting, leading a study group or a mission project. Each of these is accomplished in community and needs gifted leaders to bring their best to the effort. Again, your pastor, ministry leader, or church leadership team might be able to recommend some assessment tools and processes to help you—and you might have already completed such a process with them. If not, make that an area for development. (See the Additional Resources at the end of chapter 3 for suggestions.) If you know what your gifts, experiences, and passions are, fill in the following reflection to capture this information here.

REFLECTION

Knowing My Gifts, Experiences, and Areas of Passion

My spiritual gifts are:

My leadership experience reveals I have strengths in:

continued on the next page

My passion and my desire is to be involved in a ministry or leadership role that serves:

3. Love

You will never earn the right to fully lead people you do not love. Caring, trusting relationships form the foundation for every vibrant community. Leaders set the pace here, following Christ's example (John 13:1). Love for God, for the church, for the small group, and for the lost are trademarks of growing leaders. People tend to receive truth more readily—including correction or rebuke—when they know and feel their leaders genuinely care for them.

Listening will help you understand people and their needs. Learning will help you acquire the skills and knowledge and character to become a leader who can guide others. But without *love*, it all amounts to nothing. A familiar passage should come to mind:

> If I speak in the tongues of men and of angels, but have not love, I am only a resounding gong or a clanging cymbal. If I have the gift of prophecy and can fathom all mysteries and all knowledge, and if I have a faith that can move mountains, but have not love, I am nothing. If I give all I possess to the poor and surrender my body to the flames, but have not love, I gain nothing.
>
> Love is patient, love is kind. It does not envy, it does not boast, it is not proud. It is not rude, it is not self-seeking, it is not easily angered, it keeps no record of wrongs. Love does not delight in evil but rejoices with the truth. It always protects, always trusts, always hopes, always perseveres.
>
> Love never fails. But where there are prophecies, they will cease; where there are tongues, they will be stilled; where there is knowledge, it will pass away. For we know in part and we prophesy in part, but when perfection comes, the imperfect disappears. When I was a child, I talked like a child, I thought like a child, I reasoned like a child. When I became a man, I put childish ways behind me. Now we

see but a poor reflection as in a mirror; then we shall see face to face. Now I know in part; then I shall know fully, even as I am fully known.

And now these three remain: faith, hope and love. But the greatest of these is love.

— 1 Corinthians 13:1–13

I have often made it a point to understand the love languages of people in groups I have led. It has helped me understand—not label—people so that I and others in the group can wisely express affection, care, and concern in meaningful ways. Author, speaker, and counselor Gary Chapman lists these core love languages in his book *The Five Love Languages*:

- Words of affirmation
- Appropriate touch
- Giving gifts
- Acts of service
- Time spent together[1]

Get to know your people and genuinely express bold love to them. In most cases, they will eagerly follow your leadership. If you currently lead a group or have a good idea of who some of your group members might be, then, using the following table, take a moment to check your understanding of their love languages.

Group Member	Love Language	What would communicate love to this group member?

Leaders are lovers.

Jesus made that clear when he reinstated Peter after the disciple denied even knowing Christ during his trial. Three times, Peter claimed no relationship to Jesus, and later he was ashamed of his actions. But Jesus—and this is crucial for all leaders—is in the business of redeeming the repentant! He loves it when prodigals come home. Especially prodigal leaders! When our hearts are rightly aligned with his—even after failures, mistakes, and sins we are ashamed of—he is willing to restore us and reposition us as leaders. God is in the business of turning leadership failures into fruit. Aren't we all very glad about that timeless truth!

When Jesus restored Peter to his role and prominence as a leader in the church, he made one important demand of him. Jesus wanted to affirm that any future leadership role for Peter would require him to love the "sheep"—the people he encountered every day (certainly fellow believers but also those not yet in the fold).

Leaders are first and foremost lovers!

> When they had finished eating, Jesus said to Simon Peter, "Simon son of John, do you love me more than these?"
>
> "Yes, Lord," he said, "you know that I love you."
>
> Jesus said, "Feed my lambs."
>
> Again Jesus said, "Simon son of John, do you love me?"
>
> He answered, "Yes, Lord, you know that I love you."
>
> Jesus said, "Take care of my sheep."
>
> The third time he said to him, "Simon son of John, do you love me?"
>
> Peter was hurt because Jesus asked him the third time, "Do you love me?" He said, "Lord, you know all things; you know that I love you."
>
> Jesus said, "Feed my sheep."
>
> — John 21:15–17

Jesus is teaching a truth here that John (who was evidently standing nearby during this conversation) would write about in his first letter from exile in Patmos. John would come to understand what Peter was learning—something so central to the faith that the Holy Spirit prompted John to say it over and over throughout 1 John. Here it is:

> Dear friends, let us love one another, for love comes from God. Everyone who loves has been born of God and knows God. Whoever does not love does not know God, because God is love. . . . We love because he first loved us. Whoever claims to love God

> yet hates a brother or sister is a liar. For whoever does not love their brother or sister, whom they have seen, cannot love God, whom they have not seen. And he has given us this command: Anyone who loves God must also love their brother and sister.
>
> — 1 John 4:7–8, 19–21

In other words, loving God means loving people, and loving people means loving God. You cannot ever separate these two interdependent truths!

I hear people talk about how leaders are strategic, visionary, committed, strong, courageous, fearless, chosen by God, empowered for impact, and called to a great mission. All this is important. Yet there is an overriding practice every leader must turn into a lifestyle—love.

Don't miss the point: leaders are lovers!

4. Lead

Okay, this is obvious, I suppose. After all, leaders should . . . lead!

But I can tell you from experience that not everyone with the title or role of leader actually leads. Sounds crazy, but it's true. There are teachers who cannot teach, baseball players who cannot get a hit to save their lives, politicians who cannot govern, pastors who cannot preach, and leaders who cannot—or choose not to—lead!

Leadership can be challenging. It requires commitment and sacrifice. Jesus said, "No one who puts a hand to the plow and looks back is fit for service in the kingdom of God" (Luke 9:62). Those were hard words about full devotion spoken to an audience who did not understand the level of commitment that Christ desires and the cost of following him. Leaders prove their love for Christ by their commitment to his followers (John 21:15–19).

It is easy to have group meetings; it is harder to make disciples. Small group leaders serve in a spirit of commitment, not convenience. It takes courage, resolve, and perseverance when you are disappointed or weary. Leaders need to remain committed to the cause, to Christ, to the church, and to the people in their group.

Are you willing to do what it takes to effectively lead and care for your people?

Why Leaders Do Not Lead

- They confuse mere facilitation with leadership.
- They fear that they will appear overbearing.
- They think people don't need another "leader" in their lives.
- They fear that they are viewed as a boss.

- They think leaders are control freaks, and they refuse to become one.
- They feel spiritually inferior to some or all group members.
- They do not know the Bible as well as others do.
- They are intimidated by hard questions and difficult people.
- They believe compromise and consensus always trump leadership.
- They don't feel "visionary" enough.
- They have failed in the past and have failed some members of the group.
- They are afraid to fail.
- The cost of leadership is sometimes too high.
- They feel lonely sometimes as a leader—and who needs that?

What gets in the way of your leadership? Do you have fears that keep you from exercising leadership when you know it's the right thing to do?

REFLECTION

Leadership Fears

Which of the perspectives in the preceding list cause you to hesitate as a leader? What other perspectives not on the list concern you?

I remember talking with Russ Robinson, a ministry partner, about leadership in challenging situations and he made this statement: "We have to remember that if there is no resistance, there is no need for a leader." It was kind of a *duh* moment for me, as well as an encouragement. Leading was going to be hard; I was going to doubt my abilities; I was going to experience fear and frustration with myself and others; there would be resistance—from within and without.

Self-Leadership

This is why God calls people to take on the role and responsibilities of leaders. As a leader, you will need to excel in two areas—leading your group and leading yourself. Self-leadership is often the greater challenge. Here are some things to consider in order to lead yourself well, with truth and grace:

1. ***Face reality about your sin and weakness.*** Always, the first job of a leader is to name the reality about yourself. It is of prime importance. I have to admit that I do not like this part. It means honest reflection, humble confession, and a commitment to let it go and move ahead.
2. ***Declare your personal dignity.*** Remind yourself that in the eyes of God you are gifted, called, blessed, loved, forgiven, protected, significant, and loved (did I say that already?). This is your true identity in your relationship with Christ. Declare this daily!
3. ***Take responsibility for your own growth.*** It is up to you to go through the training, have the conversation with a mentor, reflect on the Bible, expose your mind to new ideas, network with fresh thinkers, and engage in serious debate and discussion. It's your job!
4. ***Pursue a life of simplicity and focus.*** Rid yourself of the things that tangle up your leadership—unnecessary meetings, committees, and teams; stuff that clamors for attention; people who are draining and never desire to change; the tendency to vary from your core mission. You must ruthlessly shed these distractions so that you can give maximum energy to "this one thing I do" in the moments when such focus is required.

What would you add to this list?

REFLECTION

Self-Leadership

Which of the areas in the preceding list require your immediate attention? What steps can you take to grow in this area? *(Consider these options: Read about how others face the challenge, ask mentors for help, meet with fellow*

continued on the next page

leaders to learn their strategies, consult with your coach or overseer in the ministry structure at church, pray for wisdom and courage, or develop a simple plan with accountability from others.)

Burnout sidelines many well-intentioned leaders. Listen to Paul's counsel to young Timothy: "Watch your life and doctrine closely" (1 Timothy 4:16). We need sound doctrine and sound leaders—leaders who have energy to carry out the ministry. Good leaders pay close attention to themselves; they watch their lives.

Are you emotionally, spiritually, and physically caring for yourself so that you have the energy—the capacity—to lead your group? Never sacrifice your life and family on the altar of ministry. God does not want you frazzled and exhausted while you serve others. There will be seasons of hardship and difficulty, but you cannot sustain a fruitful ministry amid frequent exhaustion and constant pressure. Here are some tips to help sustain you and avoid burnout:

- ***Set boundaries around your time and priorities.*** Learn to say no regardless of the disappointment you might cause others.
- ***Create margin in your life.*** Plan some space into your schedule—three to four unscheduled blocks of time—for fun, friends, rest, and responding to the inevitable crisis.
- ***Be diligent to replenish your reserve.*** Practice solitude and take time for celebration. Fill your tank with joy, rest, and extended community with God.

I provide more information on personal practices in chapter 3.

Participate in a Leadership Community

If you do not already meet regularly with a group of other small group leaders and ministry staff, consider forming such a group. Ask your pastoral leaders to help. A leadership community will provide you with many resources for leading more effectively. In a thriving leadership community where you are among peers and more experienced leaders, you will be able to:

- share strategies;
- tell stories about life change;
- diagnose common problems and challenges;
- learn creative ideas for discussions, prayer, and group events;
- discover fresh ideas for Bible study;
- support one another in prayer;
- become a "board of directors" for decision making;
- learn new leadership skills;
- process mistakes or failures in the safety of doing so with people who have been there;
- share resources with one another—books, training courses, online resources.

Remember what we covered earlier: *No one leads alone.* A leadership community will serve you and the church well. It will be a place to bring potential leaders and apprentice leaders who need fresh vision and encouragement for stepping up to leadership.

5. Look

We will be spending extensive time on this in chapter 4, where I will urge you to identify a rising (or potential/apprentice) leader, but the idea is that you should begin to look out for people who show potential and are willing to help you lead. I encourage you to be "looking" whenever you are engaged in church activities, classes, outings, service activities, or any environment when people gather and there is a variety of roles needed. Sometimes this will be a one-time event, but don't neglect observing who seems to be active in a leadership-type role.

REFLECTION

Listen, Learn, Love, Lead, and Look

Now that you have had some time to work through these five areas, identify one thing in each that you will learn about or work through in the next thirty days as you lead your group. If you are not currently leading, think about these areas with respect to your first meeting someday. What might serve you the best as you prepare for leadership?

Listen:

Learn:

Love:

Lead:

Look:

Note

1. Gary Chapman, *The Five Love Languages* (Moody, 2024).

CHAPTER 3

SPIRITUAL PRACTICES FOR LEADERS

PERSONAL SPIRITUAL PRACTICES FOR GROUP LEADERS

You have just completed a section designed to give you clarity in five leadership practices. Now let's look at the personal spiritual practices that will help you maintain your spiritual and emotional health as you lead others in a group.

Why Are Spiritual Practices So Important?

Spiritual practices are important because they center us. In 1 Corinthians 9:24–27, the apostle Paul says, "Do you not know that in a race all the runners run, but only one gets the prize? Run in such a way as to get the prize. Everyone who competes in the games goes into strict training. They do it to get a crown that will not last; but we do it to get a crown that will last forever. Therefore I do not run like someone running aimlessly; I do not fight like a boxer beating the air. No, I strike a blow to my body and make it my slave so that after I have preached to others, I myself will not be disqualified for the prize."

Paul here *is* comparing the Christian life to running a marathon. We run to win, reaching forward to what lies ahead, always pressing on toward the goal for the prize of the upward call of God in Christ Jesus. Like the runner, we have a goal, a strategy, and a finish line (Philippians 3:12–14). A race takes stamina, diligence, preparation, and discipline. Just as a runner would never try to enter a race without proper training, so we engage in "training" by pursuing certain practices that will enable us to endure in the race.

Spiritual "disciplines," or practices, will help you live the Christian life with authenticity, stamina, and perseverance. You practice these disciplines in preparation for hearing God's voice. They prepare you for the race you were intended to run. Hebrews 5:8 says that Jesus "learned obedience from what he suffered." Practicing the disciplines prepares you to meet God and understand his will, battle temptation, engage in loving relationships, make wise and godly decisions, love your family, and be a leader in your area of ministry.

There is great joy in being disciplined enough to finish the race. Paul wrote at the end of his life, "I have fought the good fight, I have finished the race, I have kept the faith. Now there is in store for me the crown of righteousness, which the Lord, the righteous Judge, will award to me on that day–and not only to me, but also to all who have longed for his appearing" (2 Timothy 4:7–8). Like Paul, be a leader who finishes the race well.

What Are the Spiritual Disciplines?

Dallas Willard (in *The Spirit of the Disciplines*), Richard Foster (in *Celebration of Discipline*), and Adele Calhoun (in the *Spiritual Disciplines Handbook*) have each compiled a list of spiritual disciplines and practices that they believe Christ modeled. You can refer to their books for a complete discussion (see the Additional Resources section at the end of this chapter), but spiritual disciplines are typically organized into two categories: (1) the disciplines of abstinence (or letting go) and (2) the disciplines of engagement.

Disciplines of Letting Go

These practices allow you to relinquish something in order to gain something new. You abstain from busyness in ministry, family life, and work. You stop talking for a while to hear from God. You give up buying another material possession to experience God more fully. First Peter 2:11 warns you to "abstain from sinful desires, which war against your soul." So identify what is keeping you from experiencing greater strength and perspective. Do you talk too much? Are possessions controlling you? Are you too worried about what others think? Choose disciplines that will help you become more dependent on God.

- **Solitude:** *Spending time alone to be with God.* Find a quiet place to be alone with God for a period of time. Use the Bible as a source of companionship with God. Listen to him. Remain alone and still.
- **Silence:** *Removing noisy distractions to hear from God.* Find a quiet place away from noise to hear from God. Write your thoughts and impressions as God directs your heart. Silence can occur even in the midst of noise and distraction, but you must focus your attention on your soul. This could mean talking less or talking only when necessary. And it could mean turning off the social media, the podcast, and the show you've been watching.
- **Fasting:** *Skipping a meal (or meals) to find greater nourishment from God.* Choose a period of time to go without food. Drink water and, if necessary, take vitamin supplements. Feel the pain of having an empty stomach and depend on God to fill you with his grace. (Seek the advice of your physician or qualified health provider before doing this if you have a medical condition.)
- **Frugality:** *Learning to live with less while still meeting basic needs.* Before buying something new, choose to go without or pick a less expensive alternative that will serve your basic needs. Live a simple, focused life.
- **Chastity:** *Choosing to abstain from sexual pleasures for a time (those deemed morally right in the bond of marriage) to find higher fulfillment in God.* Decide together as a couple to set aside time to go without sexual pleasures in order to experience a deeper relationship with God in prayer

- **Secrecy:** *Serving God without self-promotion so that others are unaware of your service.* Give in secret. Serve behind the scenes in a ministry that you are assured few other people will ever know about.
- **Sacrifice:** *Giving overabundantly of your resources to remind you of your dependence on Christ.* Choose to give more of your time or finances to God than you normally would.

Disciplines of Engagement

Dallas Willard writes, "The disciplines of abstinence must be counter-balanced and supplemented by disciplines of engagement (activity)."[1] Choosing to participate in activities will nurture your soul and strengthen you for the race ahead.

- **Study:** *Spending time reading the Scriptures and meditating on their meaning and importance in your life.* Scripture is your source of spiritual strength. Choose a time and a place to feed from it regularly.
- **Worship:** *Offering praise and adoration to God.* Praise of God should continually be on your lips and in your thoughts. Read psalms, hymns, spiritual songs, or sing to God daily using your favorite worship playlist. Keep praise ever before you as you think of God's activity and presence in your life.
- **Service:** *Choosing to be a humble servant as Christ was to his disciples when he washed their feet.* Consider opportunities to serve in the church and in the community. Do acts of kindness that might otherwise be overlooked (like helping someone do yard work, cleaning a house, buying groceries for someone, running an errand, and so on).
- **Prayer:** *Talking with God about your relationship with him and about the concerns of others.* Prayer involves both talking to God and listening to him. Find time to pray without the distraction of people or things. Combine your prayer time with meditation on the Scriptures in order to focus on Christ.
- **Community:** *Mutual caring and ministry in the body of Christ.* Meet regularly with other Christians to find ways to minister to others. Encourage one another.
- **Confession:** *Regularly admitting your sins to the Lord and to other trusted individuals.* As often as you are aware of sin in your life, confess it to the Lord and to those whom you may have offended.
- **Submission:** *Humbling yourself before God and others while seeking accountability in relationships.* Find faithful brothers or sisters in Christ who can lovingly hold you accountable for your actions and for your growth in Christ.

As you can see, that is a large list. It can be overwhelming. But these practices are not meant for immediate consumption, like a fast-food dinner on the way to a soccer game. Rather, they are exercises for the spiritual *life*, which is a marathon, not a sprint. As you mature and as you move through the various seasons of life, you will face challenges and opportunities that will drive you toward certain disciplines. You will find yourself learning new practices along the way, especially as you connect with other believers and leaders who are using those exercises for personal growth.

THREE PRACTICES TO INCORPORATE INTO YOUR LIFE

Of the many spiritual disciplines listed above, I want to focus on just three for you to incorporate regularly into your life—alone and with your church community.

Practice #1: Study

Reading the Bible regularly is food for the hungry soul, knowledge for the searching mind, and encouragement for the fainting heart. I have learned various ways of studying the Bible over the years, especially from other leaders and teachers in the church, both current and through the ages. Here are a few key ideas I have discovered:

- ***Study the Bible for yourself, but*** not ***just by yourself!*** Yes, you should learn to study the Bible. Take online courses; wrestle with the text; do your own work. Spend time alone digging into the Word of God. But don't stop there! Talk with others, use commentaries and reference guides. Listen to teachers on the sections or topics you are studying. Your understanding of the text is important but it could be prejudiced, narrow, or even wrong. Others in the body of Christ, especially those with teaching and scholarship gifts, can help you understand what you are reading.
- ***Never engage the text without encountering the Author.*** Too many people fall in love with the Bible and rarely find themselves in deep fellowship with the primary writer—God! When you read, expect to meet God. Expect to feel his presence and to hear his voice and to sense his life in you. Don't just let your mind be captured by the truth; let your heart be captivated by Jesus.
- ***Read the Bible for transformation, not just information.*** Read the Bible asking these questions: *How shall I now live? What difference does knowing this make?*

Then pray: *Holy Spirit, please place your finger on areas of life where I need to change and grow and turn toward God.*

Three Approaches to Reading the Bible

These methods can be used in a group or on your own. In this section, we will focus on your own Bible reading.

Approach #1: Read and Reflect

There are four movements in this approach:

1. ***Prepare your heart.*** Sit quietly or listen to worship music or read a devotional thought to open your heart to God. If you need coffee, get it. If you need a quiet place, find it. Take time to be still before God, allowing the clutter and noise to subside in your head.
2. ***Listen to the Word.*** Read the text several times. Read it slowly, repeatedly, and with a heart that seeks to meet God.
3. ***Meditate.*** Take words, phrases, or truths that emerge from the text and chew on them. Think about them. Ponder their significance. Repeat them in your head or out loud. Consider memorizing some of them. Reflect on the significance of the words. What is God saying to you, to his church, to our world?
4. ***Respond.*** Consider the action you must take. Sometimes it is simply to sit and enjoy God and his truth. Sometimes there is something to obey or someone you might need to meet with. The focus in this method is to simply commune with God and enjoy his presence. Trust the Word and the Spirit to speak.

Approach #2: Engage and Examine

In this approach, you read the text and engage with the deep and challenging phrases or truths in the passage. You not only simply meditate on the text or think about it but also study the passage rigorously. This involves four steps:

1. ***Ask questions of the text.*** What is it saying? What words are repeated or are important? Who is the audience? Who is the author? What is the purpose of the book or section? What truths or promises are listed? What is the context? What is the setting and culture?
2. ***Determine what the text meant and what it means.*** What did the author want the original audience to know? In light of their culture and setting and spiritual

condition, what was the writer communicating? Try to discern what truths, principles, or commands also apply to your life and culture today. You will likely need a study Bible, a Bible dictionary, a commentary on that book of the Bible, and other written or online resources. Ask your church leaders what they recommend for Bible study tools and resources.

3. *Search the Scriptures for similar texts, themes, or ideas.* Get a study Bible and use the concordance at the back of it or in the margins for cross-references. Start with passages in the same book of the Bible, then from the same author, and then go to other references. Where else did the writers of Scripture talk about this truth, place, idea, or character?
4. *Summarize the learning or wrestle with the tension . . . the unknown.* Given the time you have, pause and summarize what you have learned from your study. Write down conclusions or questions that you still have. How would you teach what you have learned to a ten-year-old? That is a good test.

Approach #3: Observe and Obey

The focus of this approach is heavily on the "so what"—How shall we now *live*? Here you spend less time observing and instead identify a clear command from God, knowing you can move immediately into discerning how to follow Christ in some practical way. Here are the steps:

1. *Identify six to ten verses that appear to have at least one command.* For example, "Keep in step with the Spirit" (Galatians 5:25).
2. *Use a Bible resource to get a clear definition of what the author is saying.* ("Keep in step with the Spirit" means to pay attention to what the Holy Spirit is doing as you move through your day, mindful that God's Spirit is with you.)
3. *Finally, be attentive.* Be mindful of the decisions you are pondering, relationships you are building, or promises you have made, asking the Holy Spirit to help you obey God.

Be Aware that Each Approach Has Challenges

Remember, no approach is flawless or will do full justice to all the richness of the Bible. You can spend weeks on a given passage and only scratch the surface. That is the beauty and wonder of the Bible. Though very simple and clear, enough for even a child to understand, it also holds deep truths and mysteries that take years to fully grasp, experience, and practice. The well never runs dry. So here are some cautions for each method:

- *Read and reflect.* You might be tempted to ignore challenging passages, avoid the rigor required to understand the text, or shy away from studying it later.
- *Engage and examine.* This can become an intellectual exercise if learning content and gathering information become the focus.
- *Observe and obey.* You might move too quickly to application without reflection, meeting the Author, or sitting with the truth you are reading.

Of course, you could use all three approaches in a given week. Generally, the passage of the Bible and your own growth needs will help you discern which approach is best for any given reading exercise. If you have only a few minutes, approach #1 or approach #3 might be best. If you are preparing for a lesson, approach #2 would be good, assuming you have at least an hour.

Practice #2: Prayer

A Basic Approach for Prayer

Effective leaders have vital prayer lives. So here are some guidelines to help you become a more effective leader and person of prayer. I've found them to be useful and powerful principles. First I will give you an outline for praying, then some principles for prayer from Romans 8, and then some prerequisites for answered prayer.

An Outline for Prayer: ACTS

Adoration (Psalm 100)

1. Choose one of God's attributes; praise him for his character.
2. Paraphrase a psalm.
3. Pray back a psalm.

Confession (1 John 1:9)

Take an inventory of yesterday. Is there anything there that displeases the Lord? Make a list, ask God for forgiveness, then destroy it.

Thanksgiving (Luke 17:11–19; 1 Thessalonians 5:16–18)

List your blessings, using the following categories:

1. Spiritual blessings
2. Relational blessings

3. Material blessings
4. Physical blessings

Supplication (Philippians 4:6–7; 1 John 5:14–15)

Categorize your needs under the following headings:

1. Major concerns
2. Relational concerns
3. Physical or material concerns
4. Spiritual concerns
5. Concerns regarding your character

Listen quietly—wait for the Spirit to lead and guide.

Four Principles of Prayer (Romans 8:26–29)

Paul provides some insights into prayer in Romans 8:26–29. As you read the passage and meditate on it, you will find some of the principles listed below. This information will help you understand how God responds to prayer:

1. The Holy Spirit helps you to know what and how to pray (verse 26).
2. The Holy Spirit intercedes on your behalf (verse 26).
3. God hears your heart more than the words in prayer (verse 27).
4. God always answers prayer (verses 28–29), though not always in the way you expect or according to your agenda.

There are four basic ways that God will respond to your prayers:

- *No.* Your request is not in God's will (2 Samuel 12:15–16, 22–23; Matthew 26:36–39).
- *Slow.* Your request is not in God's will at this time (Genesis 15:2–6; 21:2; John 11:3, 6, 14–15, 17, 43–44).
- *Grow.* Your motives are wrong (Numbers 14:26–45; James 4:3).
- *Go.* Your request, timing, and spiritual condition are okay. Yes! (1 Kings 18:36–39 [cf. James 5:17–18]; Acts 12:5–7, 12–17).

Prerequisites for Answered Prayer

Though it is clear from Scripture that God always answers your prayers in some manner (as mentioned above), there are also some guidelines for effective praying. Certain practices or attitudes can hinder your prayers, and in such cases God will not respond to them. The following passages reveal that you must be in a right relationship with God and with others in order for God to hear your prayers:

- **Psalm 66:18:** Harboring unconfessed sin will put a barrier between you and God.
- **1 John 3:22–23:** God hears the prayers of people who obey his commands.
- **James 4:3:** God will not hear the prayers of people who have wrong or selfish motives.
- **1 John 5:14–15:** Pray according to God's will, not according to your will.
- **Mark 11:22–24:** When you pray, ask in faith. Unbelief is a barrier to answered prayer.
- **John 15:7:** An ongoing, abiding life in Christ (having regular fellowship with him) will allow your prayers to be heard. However, when fellowship is broken, so is communication with God.
- **Luke 11:9:** Sometimes your prayers aren't answered because you do not ask. Pursue appropriate requests regularly and bring them to God.
- **Ephesians 6:18:** Praying in the Spirit (that is, under the control of the Holy Spirit) is also a prerequisite. You must also persevere in your praying.
- **Matthew 6:14–15; Mark 11:25:** If you do not forgive someone for wrongs that person has done to you, then God will not forgive you. Restored and right relationships are essential for open communication with God.
- **Philippians 4:6:** Pray with a thankful heart. If you come before God without a spirit of thankfulness, you will find that your prayers are not heard.

Four Guidelines for Prayer

1. Pray to God about everything (Philippians 4:6–7).
2. Pray consistently (1 Thessalonians 5:17).
3. Pray according to the name of Jesus—that is, according to the will of Jesus (John 16:24).
4. Pray with bold confidence (Hebrews 4:16).

The Role of the Holy Spirit

A common characteristic of great leaders in Scripture is that their lives and ministries were led by the Holy Spirit. In Ephesians 5:18–19, Paul says, "Do not get drunk on wine, which leads to debauchery. Instead, be filled with the Spirit, speaking to one another with psalms, hymns, and songs from the Spirit. Sing and make music in your heart to the Lord."

A person who is intoxicated with wine lives irresponsibly before God and others. By contrast, a person who is filled with the Holy Spirit leads a responsible, Christ-honoring life characterized by authentic relationships with God and others. How can you live a life in the Spirit? Or, better said, how can you be continually led by the Holy Spirit? As a leader, you must allow the Holy Spirit to have his way in your life. This will empower your leadership and will result in your having the fruit of the Spirit.

Remember, according to Jesus, the Spirit is your helper, your guide, and your teacher of truth (John 16:5–15). Here are two ways to be sure that you are following in the way of the Holy Spirit.

Keep in Step with the Spirit

Another way the Bible says this is to keep in step with, or walk with, the Spirit. Keeping in step with the Spirit means allowing him to control you as you read Scripture, pray, and hear God's voice. When you submit your will to God's will, the Spirit can control more of your life and direct your path.

Set Your Mind on the Things of the Spirit

Paul writes in Romans 8:6–9, "The mind governed by the flesh is death, but the mind governed by the Spirit is life and peace. The mind governed by the flesh is hostile to God; it does not submit to God's law, nor can it do so. Those who are in the realm of the flesh cannot please God. You, however, are not in the realm of the flesh but are in the realm of the Spirit, if indeed the Spirit of God lives in you. And if anyone does not have the Spirit of Christ, he does not belong to Christ."

Since the Spirit of God already dwells in you, you simply need to yield yourself to him and allow him to take control of your life. Focusing on the things of the Spirit means paying attention to God-honoring relationships, decisions, conversations, thoughts, and activities.

Paul explains in Galatians 5:22–23 that a life lived in the Spirit, with obedience to Christ's commands, will yield the fruit of the Spirit—"love, joy, peace, forbearance, kindness, goodness, faithfulness, gentleness and self-control." However, when you are not yielded to the Spirit, you either quench the Spirit (1 Thessalonians 5:19) by ignoring the Word of God or grieve the Spirit (Ephesians 4:30) by bringing resentment and anger to relationships. Sin always pours water on the fire of the Holy Spirit.

REFLECTION

By applying the principles we've just discussed, you can live a Spirit-filled life and allow God to work through you to be an effective leader. To learn more about the work of the Spirit in the life of a leader and in the life of believers, read the following passages. You might also want to work through some of these as a small group to encourage others to live a life in the Spirit.

- **1 Corinthians 12:13:** The baptism of the Holy Spirit.
- **Romans 8:11; 1 Corinthians 3:16; 2 Timothy 1:14:** The indwelling ministry of the Holy Spirit.
- **Acts 4:8, 31; Ephesians 5:18:** The filling ministry of the Holy Spirit.
- **John 16:7–11:** The convicting ministry of the Holy Spirit.
- **John 3:3–6; Titus 3:5–6:** The regenerating ministry of the Holy Spirit.
- **1 Corinthians 2:12–16; 1 John 4:13; 5:7–8:** The reassuring ministry of the Holy Spirit.
- **Romans 8:11–12; 2 Corinthians 3:18; 2 Thessalonians 2:13:** The sanctifying ministry of the Holy Spirit.
- **John 16:13; 1 Corinthians 2:13:** The teaching ministry of the Holy Spirit.
- **Romans 8:26:** The intercessory ministry of the Holy Spirit.
- **Luke 4:14, 18–19; Acts 1:8; Romans 15:13, 19:** The empowering ministry of the Holy Spirit.
- **John 14:16:** The comforting ministry of the Holy Spirit.
- **John 16:7:** The convicting work of the Holy Spirit.
- **Acts 9:31:** The encouraging work of the Holy Spirit.
- **Galatians 5:16–26; Ephesians 5:18:** The believer's responsibility to be filled with the Holy Spirit.

Practice #3: Community

Relational integrity stems directly from authentic communal engagement. We are, at some level, the product of our communities. Living with others reveals our pride and ego, yet it also gives us opportunities to be "for" others and share in their lives. This practice keeps leaders from thinking too highly of themselves and from self-absorption.

You might be thinking, *I lead a small group, so I have community already.* If the group you are leading provides you with a deeply connected, trust-filled, grace-based, safe environment in which you can be yourself and share your struggles, great! If not, you need to find a couple of people who understand you well. And even if your group is great (as many of mine have been through the years), there is often the need to enjoy some community life with other leaders who know the joys and heartaches of leadership.

Jesus connected more deeply with Peter, James, and John. Paul often had one or two close partners with him, doing ministry and sharing life (Titus, Luke, Timothy, Priscilla and Aquila). So what about you?

A Band of Brothers, a Society of Sisters

Every leader needs a relational support network. Your life in an authentic community will provide the care, the opportunities for personal growth, and the place to simply "be" that you need. When leaders fail to experience such a community—whether in the group they lead or with some other group leaders—they will eventually find their souls withering and their hearts becoming despondent.

For many leaders, this is usually a men's or women's group. But it can also be a mixed group or a couples' group. The key is what you find there. Here are some questions for you, as a leader seeking community, to ask about such a group:

1. Does the group treat you as a leader in a role or as a person in relationship? *(You want the latter.)*
2. Is this a place where you find safety and friendship?
3. Does the community offer accountability that is not judgmental but rather inspirational, where you come alongside one another to help each other stay the course and work through sin or brokenness?
4. Can you share frustrations about ministry challenges without fear that others in the group will become discouraged with the church?
5. Are there one or two others in the group who could be close spiritual friends—people with whom you could share deeply and confess the deeper personal needs and faults you have?
6. Is there a culture of grace and truth that, over time, will allow you to walk more closely with Christ and others?
7. Do others in the group understand the specific needs, disappointments, and frustrations that accompany leadership in a spiritual setting?

Working through these questions will help you and potential members of the group create the environment necessary for real community.

REFLECTION

My Personal Community

Take a few moments to pray about who might be in your inner circle of fellow leaders—people with whom you can share life and speak the truth in love.

No One Leads Alone

"No one stands alone!" is a mantra I have championed for years. Group life matters. We want a place in community for everyone. But we should add, "No one leads alone!" Authentic leadership requires a leader to rely on others, empower others, and learn from others.

In addition to having a place in community for yourself, here are insights about authentic, communal leadership that will prevent you from becoming a lone ranger leader.

Authentic Leaders Allow Others to "Outperform" Them

"God save us from *becoming* know-it-all leaders," said Dave Fleming. Such leaders have the "solo shepherd" syndrome and cripple the body instead of allowing each part to do its work (Ephesians 4:15–16). In groups, we draw out the giftedness and experience of others, releasing them into ministry. Everyone in the circle has something to offer. Sadly, some leaders fear that members will outperform them. But this never worried Jesus—in fact, it was his desire. His followers were to do "even greater things than these," he said in John 14:12. The best leaders empower others to outperform them and can celebrate when that happens.

Authentic Leaders Align the Group's Vision with the Church's Mission

Almost as bad as know-it-all leaders are leave-me-alone leaders. Some small group leaders want no coaching or accountability. But group leaders must understand their role is delegated to them by the people with spiritual authority in the church who, in turn, must give an account to Christ for the condition of the flock. Small groups exist to mobilize members *to carry out the ministry of the local church.* It is essential that your group aligns its specific purpose (Bible study, personal growth, recovery, and so on) with the overall mission of the church.

Authentic Leaders Learn from Failure

Watch out for the I-can-fix-it-alone leader. In ministry, failure is fatal when a leader will not process it with others. Instead, a leader should name the failure and take steps to process the experience with others, building hope for future ministry success. For example, imagine you are a group leader in student ministry who takes the members to a homeless shelter without informing parents. You can say to parents later, "I allowed my passion for giving students a look at the plight of the homeless to exceed my discernment in communicating to you. Please forgive me." Own your mistake and design a process that will build trust as you go forward with your group. Don't be tempted to destroy the power of community by being alone or by leading alone. It's dangerous for you and a deadly example for your small group to follow.

REFLECTION

My Leadership

As you think of your leadership role, how will you become a communal leader so you never lead alone and so you have a group to help you along the way?

ADDITIONAL RESOURCES

On Leadership

Warren Bennis and Burt Nanus, *Leaders: The Strategies for Taking Charge* (Harper and Row, 1985). Bennis and Nanus focus on managing yourself, creating vision, communicating your vision, developing trust, and organizational management. It is a book that emphasizes strategies for personal and organizational leadership.

Robert Clinton, *The Making of a Leader* (NavPress, 2012). Probably the best book on Christian leadership and the role of the Spirit. Clinton emphasizes the six stages of leadership development and establishes checkpoints to clarify where you are in each stage of the process. Also very helpful for maturing new leaders under your care.

Roberta Hestenes, *Using the Bible in Groups* (Westminster, 1985). A classic on how to do group Bible study and discussion.

J. Oswald Sanders, *Spiritual Leadership* (Moody, 1994). Sanders writes that spiritual leadership is the blending of natural and spiritual qualities. His book is a Christian classic. Though a little dated and written primarily to men, it is a thorough, biblically principled book on Christian leadership.

On Prayer

E. M. Bounds, *Power Through Prayer* (Moody, 2011). This is a classic for motivating your prayer life.

Richard Foster, *Prayer: Finding the Heart's True Home* (HarperOne, 2002). Show how to grow in a living relationship with God, moving beyond routine words into authentic communion with him. Foster describes many forms of prayer and shows how you can experience deeper intimacy with God through listening, surrender, and trust.

On the Holy Spirit

J. I. Packer, *Keep in Step with the Spirit* (Baker, 2005). Packer emphasizes that Christians grow spiritually by actively cooperating with the Spirit through repentance, faith, and disciplined living according to Scripture.

Charles Swindoll, *Flying Closer to the Flame* (Word, 1993). Reveals how to pursue God wholeheartedly rather than settling for comfortable or routine faith. Swindoll challenges Christians to move closer to God's presence—like a moth drawn to a flame—where true transformation, intimacy, and purpose are found.

On Spiritual Gifts Assessments

Bruce Bugbee, Don Cousins, and Wendy Seidman, *Network Series: Assessment, Leader's Guide, Participant Guide* (Authors, 2005). Teaching and materials for leaders and participants needed to help members discovers their gifts, understand how they can use them in the body of Christ, and better understand how God created them to love and serve others.

On Evangelism

M. Scott Boren, *Missional Small Groups* (Baker, 2010). Boren explains that small groups are meant to be communities that join God's mission. When groups focus on shared life, listening to the Spirit, and engaging their neighborhoods, they become spaces where people grow and participate in God's redemptive work together.

Rebecca Pippert, *Out of the Saltshaker* (Intervarsity, 1999). Pippert teaches that evangelism is not a program or event but a natural lifestyle that grows out of authentic relationships with people and a genuine love for them.

Lee Strobel, *The Case for Christ* (Zondervan, 2016). Through interviews with scholars and experts, Strobel, a former *Chicago Tribune* legal journalist, concludes that the biblical claims about Christ are historically credible and intellectually compelling.

On Spiritual Disciplines

Adele Calhoun, *Spiritual Disciplines Handbook* (IVP Books, 2015). A practical guide that explains dozens of Christian spiritual disciplines and how they help believers open their lives to God's transforming presence. The book describes the purpose, practice, and benefits of each discipline.

John Ortberg, *The Life You've Always Wanted* (Zondervan, 2015). Ortberg teaches that spiritual transformation doesn't happen through trying harder but through practicing spiritual disciplines that open your life to God's work. Practices such as habits, solitude, prayer, and service help you live with deeper joy, freedom, and Christlike character.

Dallas Willard, *The Spirit of the Disciplines* (HarperOne, 1994). Philosopher and theologian Dallas Willard teaches that spiritual disciplines are not ways to earn God's favor but practices that train you to live in the reality of God's kingdom, becoming gradually transformed to be like Jesus from the inside out.

Note

1. Dallas Willard, *The Spirit of the Disciplines* (HarperOne, 1994).

CHAPTER 4

DEVELOPING YOUR APPRENTICE

SHARED LEADERSHIP

Now that you have a clearer picture of your role as a small group leader, it is time to prepare to build your leadership team. In order to assure that nobody stands alone in your church, you will need more groups, and that means more leaders. You were given a leadership baton, and the time will come for you to pass it to—or share it with—another. You will teach leadership lessons to your apprentice through practical on-the-job experiences in the small group.

In Exodus 18:18, Jethro said to Moses, his burnt-out and overworked son-in-law, "You and these people who come to you will only wear yourselves out. The work is too heavy for you; you cannot handle it alone." Mutual leadership is a biblical pattern *and* a practical necessity. So, in this chapter, you will discover how to identify and develop your apprentice(s), giving them the skills and experiences needed to move forward.

You will learn to delegate responsibilities to the person you are developing. In doing so, you will see the fruit of your labor as you watch new leaders emerge from your group to guide others in the church toward spiritual growth. By developing apprentice leaders, you will build a transformational community through your church.

Here is the flow of apprentice development that we will discuss in this chapter: (1) affirm the *need*, (2) *find* a candidate, (3) assess baseline *character* and *skills*, (4) begin to *develop* this rising leader, and (5) recognize this is a process of passing through *stages* of growth along the way. I hope you will embrace the mantra, "No one leads alone!"

WHY DO YOU NEED AN APPRENTICE LEADER—SOONER THAN LATER?

If you look at the flow of Scripture through "leadership eyes," you will notice a pattern that emerges. Not long after someone rises up (or is chosen), the existing leader begins to develop or include that person in the learning and practice of kingdom ministry. Notice the prophetic mentoring between Elijah and Elisha, Jesus and the Twelve, Barnabas and Paul, Paul and Timothy, Paul and Priscilla with Acquila—to name a few popular examples.

While some time may elapse, identifying rising leaders happens *sooner* rather than later. Early on, not long after the ministry is launching and growing, there is intentionality in choosing ministry co-leaders, partners, or some functional shared leadership. In the same way, the sooner you, as the group leader, begin to share aspects of leading a group, the more likely potential apprentices will begin to appear (though this is not *always* the case). The sooner you gradually share responsibilities and include others in group leadership processes and practices, the sooner it becomes a common group value and practice.

The vitality and effectiveness of any local church is directly related to the quality of its leadership. The ministry of group life flourishes when churches emphasize the ongoing development of leaders in the body. It is the church's responsibility to identify and develop new leaders in order to accomplish the mission of the gospel and shepherd people. As mentioned, Jesus modeled this with the twelve disciples, and Paul exhorted Timothy to model this as well (2 Timothy 2:2).

I am a firm believer in mobilizing and building up the body of Christ so that each member can accomplish the ministry God has given them, as described in Ephesians 4:12. It is the duty and privilege of all small group leaders to train up a new generation of leaders and pass the baton effectively. The future hangs in the balance. So work together as a team—leaders, coaches, ministry builders—to raise up new leaders for service in the kingdom.

REFLECTION

Your Leadership Legacy

Quickly read through Romans 16:1–16. There are lots of hard names to pronounce, but what else do you observe? What does this tell you about Paul and his approach to ministry?

What might your list look like someday? How many leaders will you leave in your wake?

What's the Difference Between an Apprentice and an Assistant Leader?

Your apprentice is one who will lead after you, not a person to whom you delegate unwanted details, projects, and "administrivia." Here is a summary of the difference:

An Apprentice	An Assistant
Will be a leader someday	Will always support another leader
Shares responsibilities	Avoids responsibility
Engages in the same ministry as the leader	Does what the leader does not want to do
Helps lead the meeting	Only helps prepare for the meeting
Focuses on leadership skills	Focuses on logistics
Has their eyes on the vision	Has their head in the details

You and your apprentice are *partners* in ministry, and the relationship should reflect that as you prepare for meetings, lead meetings, and share responsibilities between meetings.

Note that assistant leaders are not bad people, or disobedient to a call, or rebelling against the church vision. Not everyone is made for leading a group; thus, being a faithful helper to another leader is an important (and needed) role in many cases. However, it is hard to build and launch a new group from your group by simply employing an assistant. You need a rising *apprentice* who is actively preparing to lead or co-lead a group.

How Do You Find Potential Apprentices?

Here is a brief list of what to look for in an apprentice:

- Look for group members who take the group seriously.
- Consider people who challenge your leadership. They may be potential leaders who are frustrated because they have no opportunity to lead.
- Look for gifted people whom you can recognize and affirm.
- Pray regularly for new apprentices (Luke 6:12–16).
- Look for people who embrace the small group vision.
- Observe people in your ministry as they perform tasks or work with people. Give them additional ministry opportunities and responsibilities to see if perhaps they have some leadership potential.

In addition, look for people who exhibit the following spiritual, emotional, and social qualifications:

Spiritual Qualifications

- Is it evident that God is working in their life?
- Are they "self-feeders"? (Do they consistently nurture their own spiritual growth through time in God's Word and in prayer?)
- Are they eager to learn? (Do they actively participate in spiritual discussions?)
- Do they share the vision of small groups in the church?

Emotional Qualifications

- Are they secure enough to be vulnerable and honest with the group?
- Are they emotionally stable? (Are they aware of their own strengths and weaknesses and not subject to mood swings that affect the group dynamic?)
- How do they respond to confrontation about their need for character growth? Defensively? Humbly?

Social Qualifications

- Do they openly participate without dominating the discussion?
- Are they able to listen to others in a caring way?
- Are they able to facilitate discussion?

REFLECTION

Identifying an Apprentice

List the names of some potential leaders. Think about group members, friends, people taking the same classes with you at church, ministry team participants, new believers who have leadership backgrounds in education or the marketplace, coworkers, teammates in sports, and so on.

1.

2.

3.

4.

5.

How Do You Overcome the Typical Objections from Potential Leaders?

Objection #1: "I just don't have the time."

People make time for things they consider important, so share the importance of apprentice leadership in the body of Christ. Cast a vision for the life change that can occur as they participate in this new role as an apprentice.

Objection #2: "I don't have the gift of leadership."

Encourage people by reminding them that leadership is mostly character. It takes time to develop character and competence. If you believe someone has the basic character qualities of a potential leader, assure them that you will make sure they get the appropriate training so they have the skills they need to be effective.

Objection #3: "I'm not the leadership type."

Explore what they mean by "leadership type." They may have a definition of leadership that is not biblical. They may view a leader as someone who is in charge and in control as opposed to someone who can facilitate life change by caring for, discipling, and loving others.

How Do You Confirm You Have the Right Person as a Potential Apprentice?

1. Make sure they meet your ministry leaders at the church.
2. Check with others who have ministered with them or who know them.
3. Confirm that they have a teachable spirit and are willing to learn.

What If You Have Trouble Finding an Apprentice?

Recruiting apprentice leaders is a spiritual battle. The evil one is not pleased when we develop new leaders who can impact the body of Christ and reach the world with the gospel. Though other group leaders, "coaches," and ministry leaders can aid you in helping you choose your apprentice, the role of the Holy Spirit and prayer is essential. Developing an apprentice is as important as evangelism, because an apprentice will go on someday to create group life that will reach out to believers and spiritual seekers.

What Information Does a Potential Apprentice Need?

1. *Describe the role of a group leader.* Assure the potential apprentice that they are not expected to fulfill the job description requirements to the same degree that a leader would. Remember, the role they are considering is that of a developing leader.
2. *Provide a clear picture of the time frame for apprentice development.* An apprentice will need approximately five to six meetings for development before they can lead a small group

on their own. This varies depending on the needs of a given ministry, the maturity of the apprentice, and how frequently a group meets (e.g., weekly, twice monthly, monthly).

3. ***Explain that adequate training and resources are available for an apprentice's growth and encouragement.***
4. ***Communicate the vision and values of the small group ministry.*** The apprentice should attend any required training events of the church. If your church has a formal membership requirement for leaders and the person is not yet affirmed as a participating member in the church, work with your church leadership to help the person enter the process.

REFLECTION

What Are My Concerns About Developing an Apprentice?

It is sometimes difficult to find an apprentice—someone who is willing to step up into a leadership development role. Perhaps you need to look for *people* instead of *leaders* when considering potential apprentices. We leaders—especially if we've been at it a while—tend to look at others through the lenses of our own gifts, abilities, and experiences as leaders and quickly disqualify people. So take a moment to read through the following thoughts and questions and see if they provoke some fresh thinking and strategies on your part.

- Recall your first real leadership role—at work, church, home, or school—and try to remember what that felt like. Perhaps it was scary or overwhelming. Did you succeed? Fail? Learn a lot along the way?
- Did someone take a risk by putting you in leadership? Did you have the freedom to fail?
- Maybe you stepped up to lead a group. That took some courage and was a bit risky—for you, the church, and the group! Have you since lost your boldness? What would it take to be courageous again and make the ask?
- What *is* keeping you from making a bold ask, inviting someone to share leadership with you and to move toward their own leadership role someday?
- Perhaps you need help from your church staff or your ministry leader. Don't be afraid to ask. They will pray with you and help you create a strategy for finding and developing a future leader.

What Are Some Tips for Developing an Apprentice Leader?

1. ***Work through this book with your apprentice.*** Select various sections and discuss how the two of you can apply the principles and information to your group.
2. ***Continue to model group leadership to your apprentice.*** Your example is probably the only example of small group leadership your apprentice has ever seen.
3. ***Allow your apprentice to lead.*** Delegate areas of responsibility to him or her.
4. ***Make sure that you and your apprentice are regularly giving feedback to one another.*** When your apprentice leads a portion of the meeting, provide them with feedback, and vice versa. Create a list of questions with which to evaluate one another.
5. ***Pray regularly with your apprentice for their personal needs and leadership development.***
6. ***Help your apprentice determine what types of skill training would best fit in their stage of development.*** Work with your team of group leaders, coaches, or other ministry leaders to direct your apprentice to the right training opportunities.
7. ***Bring your apprentice with you whenever you are involved in ministry.*** If you are going to visit someone who is sick, bring your apprentice. If you are planning to attend a ministry meeting, make sure your apprentice comes with you. Remember to involve your apprentice in meetings with your coach or staff leadership at the church.
8. ***Help your apprentice find a ministry partner and future apprentice.*** You can never have too many apprentices. For you to develop more new groups and more leaders, you will need to identify new apprentice leaders.
9. ***Use the Apprenticeship Planner (page 68).*** This will help you think through how you will work with your apprentice each month. The planner is divided into four sections: (1) the apprentice's involvement in meetings, (2) the apprentice's work with members, (3) the apprentice's personal development, and (4) long-term planning and goals. Sit down each month and work through the planner together.
10. ***Walk your apprentice through the process of becoming a participating member of the church, if that is required.***

MATERIAL TO USE WHEN WORKING WITH YOUR APPRENTICE LEADER

The following material will be helpful when you find and begin meeting with an apprentice. Have the person read and work through the content with you. Since your apprentice is going to be a leader someday, make sure they have a copy of *How to Lead a Life-Changing Small Group.*

If I Become an Apprentice, What Can I Expect?

The journey from apprentice to leader is an exciting and challenging experience. In the apprentice development process, you will need to pay attention to certain rules of the road, rites of passage, and responsibilities given to you.

Rules of the Road (Qualifications)

Small group leadership is essentially the combination of expressed character and applied skills:

Character	Skills
Must be developed	Can be provided
Takes time	Takes practice and time
Can disqualify you from leadership	Can delay you from leadership
Involves your relationship to God and others	Involves your performance of a task
Is an inward measure	Are outward measures
Is tested in adversity but developed in quiet times	Are practiced in quiet times but tested in adversity

Here are a few biblical guidelines for baseline character and skills:

Baseline Character	Baseline Skills
Serve (Mark 10:35–45)	Able to teach and manage responsibilities (1 Timothy 3:1–7)
Love (John 13:34–35)	Able to stand up for sound doctrine (Titus 1:9)
Integrity (1 Timothy 3:1–7)	Lead with diligence (Romans 12:8)
Fruit-bearing (Galatians 5:22–23)	Shepherd with eagerness (1 Peter 5:1–4)

You are not expected to have developed all of these character traits by the time you become a small group leader. However, make it your *aim* to develop them as you mature in Christ.

Rites of Passage (Stages of Apprentice Development)

The three stages of apprentice development mirror the stages of early life. I've named the steps *dependence*, *independence*, and *interdependence*, and they mirror the stages of infancy, adolescence, and adulthood. As an apprentice, you may experience them this way:

Stage 1: Dependence (Infancy)

- You explore leadership.
- You learn all you can.
- You become an observer.
- You rely on the leader.
- You develop a servant's heart.
- You exhibit strong dependence on the group.

Stage 2: Independence (Adolescence)

- You feel you can lead better than the leader can (and that might be true at times).
- You think you don't need the group (a bad assumption).
- You think you don't need support from the group leader anymore (wrong).
- You are learning the leader's role.

Caution: Though this is a normal stage in development, it is also the most dangerous, for it is the time when you think you are better than your leader and can easily lead the group. This feeling should be an indication that you're ready to take on more responsibility for the group and share more directly in the leadership of it. Your goal is not to *stay* in this stage of independence. In Christ, we are to become dependent on one another. You must seek to move toward the third stage—interdependence.

Stage 3: Interdependence (Adulthood)

- You have earned the respect of the group. You respect the group.
- You need the group to affirm your leadership. The group needs you.
- You work with your leader as a team. You share ownership with your leader.
- You have combined the servant's heart with the leader's role.

Note: At this stage, you may be preparing to lead your own group. Don't be surprised if feelings of ambivalence, uncertainty, fear, and inadequacy arise. This is normal and healthy. As a matter of fact, these feelings will give you the humility you need to become a leader. That they come is an indication that you are ready to launch out, lead, and be further challenged in your spiritual growth.

Responsibilities (Five Core Practices of an Apprentice Leader)

Note to apprentices: These are the same leadership practices as for a small group leader but with a different focus as you develop your leadership abilities.

1. Listen

Listen to what the group leader is saying, how they are saying it, how they guide the discussion, and how they respond to members. Practice your own listening skills as you hear people in the group talking. What are they really saying with their facial expressions, posture, tone of voice, and choice of words? Listen to the words, but listen *beyond* the words. Debrief with the group leader to see if you both had the same experience.

2. Love

Love and support your leader and your group. Do all you can to be an example of the love of Christ toward your group members by taking an active role in loving and caring for them. Work with your leader to share the care load in the group. There are people you can call, pray for (and with), and listen to.

3. Learn

Learn from what your leader *does* and *does not* do. Talk with your leader and debrief after each meeting, discussing the pros and cons of the process. At this point, leadership is both caught and taught. Take advantage of skill training as it is offered or recommended.

4. Lead

Ask your leader to give you experience in leading the group. Begin by leading the prayer time or facilitating the dialogue for one or two discussion questions. Over time, take more ownership and leadership in the group. You will become a better leader by practicing leadership skills in a live setting, and now is the best time to do that. You should be leading after five to six meetings of becoming an apprentice, depending on your experience and background. So take advantage of this time to grow and master a variety of skills.

5. Look

As you lead, begin to look for your own potential apprentices! In fact, do this throughout your ministry as an apprentice. Ask yourself questions like these:

- *Who might have leadership potential?*
- *Who has a servant's heart?*
- *Who is willing to learn?*
- *Do I have friends who are not participating in group life at the church?*

Apprentice Development Planner

Leaders and apprentices: Consider working through the following planner together. Lay out a strategy for meetings, for content you will cover, for how you will work with group members, and so on. It's not complicated but will require some intentionality on your part.

APPRENTICESHIP PLANNER

Month	Meetings	Members	Personal Development	Long-Term Planning

ADDITIONAL RESOURCES

J. Robert Clinton and Paul D. Stanley, *Connecting* (NavPress, 1992). This book focuses on various kinds of mentoring relationships and how to develop them.

Bill Donahue and Greg Bowman, *Coaching Life-Changing Small Group Leaders* (Zondervan, 2012). This presents a framework for coaching small group leaders in a way that provides care, support, and leadership development.

Bill George, *True North* (Jossey-Bass, 2007). This resource, and the workbook that goes with it, are great tools for developing leaders at every level and include exercises for leaders to work through.

John Maxwell, *Developing the Leaders Around You* (Nelson, 1995). Maxwell gives very practical guidelines and strategies for investing in and equipping the potential leaders you are working with.

CHAPTER 5

CREATING A CULTURE FOR SPIRITUAL GROWTH IN YOUR GROUP

NOT-SO-GREAT EXPECTATIONS

We previously discussed the importance of intentional spiritual practices for you as a leader. Now let's focus on the growth culture of your group. People have various expectations and ideas when it comes to group success. Everyone has their own way of defining what the optimal group is like. Each person comes with a list—sometimes in their subconscious—of what the group should be and do. Your responsibility as a leader is to engage the group in a process of describing group health and coming to some consensus about how to achieve it together.

You might be asking, "What kind of atmosphere or culture must exist in a group or any small community of people so they can work together, respect one another, grow personally, and accomplish the mission to which they feel called?"

This is what we will uncover in this chapter. We will first talk about environment—spiritual greenhouses—and then address the process that encourages transformation, the values that shape a group, and the structures that will help produce growth. You will learn (1) how to create and cast a vision for your group, (2) the major components of group growth, (3) communication patterns, (4) the life stages through which the group will pass, and (5) how to design a covenant or ground rules that describe your commitment to one another.

BUILDING SPIRITUAL GREENHOUSES (ENVIRONMENT)

Picture a greenhouse, a place where plants are nurtured toward growth and protected from harsh elements. Nurturing people in a group setting is similar because both plants and humans are organisms that respond to their environment as they grow.

Effective greenhouses have three basic characteristics. First, there is a *process* for growing plants. It involves planting them in rich soil, watering regularly, applying nutritious fertilizer, and pruning away bad growth or removing weeds.

Second, there is a *structure* to protect the growth process from destructive forces. Wind, excess heat, heavy rains, extreme cold, and interaction with people or animals can create erosion, limit growth, or even cause the death of the plants. Usually, the structure is not attractive, and neither is it the focal point, yet it is essential. Primarily made of glass, plastic, and metal, the structure protects the environment from destructive outside forces.

Third, there is the *growth* of the plants. Growth is expected in the greenhouse, and maturity is essential if the plants are to one day be removed into other, less sheltered environments for which they were intended.

Process, structure, and growth. The first two are necessary if the third is to take place. Even with the right process and structure, some plants never reach their potential. They may barely grow or wither and die. We do not control the mysterious nature of the plants themselves. They may have a disease, or have a faulty internal structure, or be unreceptive to the nutrients provided. We usually do not know the reason why growth does not occur.

What Could Your Group Become?

Your group is a greenhouse, not a factory. The inputs do not guarantee the outputs. Paul made this point when writing to the church in Corinth: "I planted the seed, Apollos watered it, but God has been making it grow" (1 Corinthians 3:6). Paul could have easily said, "We worked the process within the structure of our ministry framework and design, but the mysteries of growth lie within each person as God works in them."

We do our best, with God's help, to create environments conducive to growth.

In the spiritual greenhouse of a small group, there exists the same three components found in a botanical greenhouse: *process*, *structure*, and *growth*. When a real greenhouse is effective, the result is not just the growth of individual plants and flowers but also the creation of beautiful landscapes, gardens, and parks.

We don't begin with a vision for a greenhouse. We have a vision for a world filled with beautiful landscapes, parks, and gardens. We build greenhouses with process, structure, and growth because we want to serve a greater, more majestic purpose—beauty.

The spiritual greenhouse we call a small group is similar. It's not our vision to have a small group; it's our vision to see Christ build his church, populated with people who love him, love his creation, love each other, and love people who don't yet know his love and grace. We envision a world filled with justice, hope, redemption, care, joy, love, and beauty. We launch small groups as environments to nurture the growth of people, with God's help and power, who will enter that world we long to create.

Your group needs a vision for what it can be to change the world!

In chapter 1, you were instructed to think through your own vision. Now it is time to use that material, and the content in this chapter, to help your members embrace a vision for the entire group. We will then move to process, structure, and growth within the group.

REFLECTION

Questions to Ponder About Your Group

- What will your group look like in a year? How will it be different?
- What do you hope you will become as you work within the spiritual greenhouse of group life, asking God to bring maturity and growth?
- How might the world be different because of your group?
- What will your group look like when it is functioning well?
- Jesus invited us into kingdom life—his way of living by God's values, love and mission (John 17). What does that mean? Do you want to learn from Jesus and be like him for the sake of the world—to be in union and oneness with God through Jesus?

Forming and Communicating a Vision for Your Group

A vision is inspiring. It's a picture of a desired future—what you want to become. A vision should be compelling and something around which your group can rally. For example, a group's vision might be expressed like this: "To become a Christlike community that is growing spiritually in God's Word, relationally through mutual engagement, emotionally through authentic communication, and numerically by adding new people to our group."

A vision must be:

- **Concise:** It takes work to articulate a vision that can be stated in a sentence or two. This forces your group to choose very specific words to define the vision. Long, drawn out vision statements are hard to remember and difficult to communicate.
- **Clear:** Make sure your vision has clarity and is easily understood. For example, in the vision statement above, it's clear that the group wants to grow relationally and add members to their group.
- **Consistent:** Is the vision consistent with the overall mission of the church? Your group's vision statement should relate directly to the purpose of the church.
- **Compelling:** Is your vision statement something you can sink your teeth into? Is it something worth rallying around? Does it reflect the passion of the group and draw others to it?

- **Collaborative:** Was the vision statement developed in collaboration with the group? It's important to work *with* your group members (or at least the regular attendees) to create a vision statement that reflects the values of the group as a whole. The more your group members own the vision, the more they will make a commitment to it. Without a vision, your group will wander aimlessly and lack a clear purpose.

REFLECTION

Group Vision

What kind of group do you want to become as you accomplish your purpose? Take some time (perhaps a few minutes each meeting for two or three meetings) to shape your vision.

Our Vision:

THE THREE ESSENTIALS FOR CREATING SPIRITUAL GREENHOUSES

1. The Process: Living Our Group Values

All groups operate according to certain values and expectations. Often these go unspoken or unwritten. So, in order to foster open communication and clarity about the purpose and values of the group, put down your core values in writing.

Before you go further, note that values are not the same as practices. For example, regular Bible reading is a practice—something you *do*, not a value. A value, on the other hand, is a principle or belief. Authenticity is a value; telling each other the truth is a practice.

What follows are key values for small group relationships. This is only a sample set of values. You and your group should create your own list with the kinds of values central to your group. Again, consider your ministry when deciding on the right approach for your group. The important thing is that your members are committed to growing in interpersonal relationships and maturity in Christ. Here are some examples of values:

- **Affirmation:** It is important to create an atmosphere in which group members affirm and encourage one another, build each other up in Christ, and help each other grow.
- **Availability:** Group members should be available to each other. Each member should be willing to make their resources (time, attention, insights, as well as material resources) available to the other members in the group in order to meet needs and serve one another.
- **Prayerfulness:** This is a posture of openness with God and listening for his voice. Practicing this posture means the group comes together before God to praise, ask, confess, and thank him for all he has done. This encourages the members to be humble, knowing that all comes from God.
- **Openness:** Openness in the relationships within the group promotes honesty and an ease of sharing feelings, struggles, joys, and hurts. Reaching the goal of authentic relationships begins with being open with each other and with opening the group to new members. (Some may call this vulnerability.)
- **Honesty:** The desire to be honest with each other is critical to authentic relationships. In order to build trust in the group, members must speak the truth in love to one another.
- **Safety:** Honest, open relationships must be safeguarded with an agreement that what is said in the group will remain confidential, that opinions will be respected, and that differences will be allowed.
- **Confidentiality:** As part of the value of safety, confidentiality promotes openness by promising that whatever is shared within the confines of the group will not be repeated elsewhere.
- **Sensitivity:** A commitment to being sensitive and aware to the needs, feelings, backgrounds, and current situations of all members will help build relationships in the group.
- **Accountability:** In authentic relationships, accountability is voluntary submission to another member (or other members) for support, encouragement, and help in a particular area of life. This gives the members some responsibility for assisting another member in that area.

- **An Evangelistic Heart:** As considered from a group perspective, a heart for people who need Jesus means being committed to expanding the community of believers through such things as sharing the gospel with others, inviting people into the group, or other types of outreach and relational connections.
- **Group Growth:** Having your group grow and eventually give life to a new group enables it to carry out the vision of seeing more people connected in Christian community, growing in their relationship with Christ.
- **Mutual Care:** Showing care to one another in the group and to others is an expression of Christ's love. A caring group is often a safe group for new people. Care and compassion are essential for group life.
- **Help:** Meeting practical needs in the group by sharing gifts and abilities is a way to support one another. Helping each other with doing taxes, moving furniture, babysitting, making meals, doing homework, doing yard work, repairing cars, meeting financial challenges, and so on communicates the group cares about all its members' needs, not just crises or illnesses.
- **Authenticity:** Being real with one another opens the group to greater truthfulness in discussions and creates an environment of respect. It promotes humility and safety.

Choose four to six of these values or create your own. (You might want all of these in your group, but this list is too long, so try to develop four to six core values.) You did some work on this in chapter 1, so now process this further on your own and then with your group.

REFLECTION

Crafting Your Values

1. Ask each member to list (or choose from a list like the one provided) the three values that matter most in order for the group to function well. Remember, these are values, which describe the relational environment you want for the group.
2. Gather all the lists and see what four to six values are most common or most essential.

continued on the next page

3. Define each value in two or three sentences. You can assign this to groups of two, asking each pair to take one value, define it, and then share it with the entire group for revisions and input.
4. Create a final list of four to six core values with brief definitions that all members have at least 80 percent agreement with (every definition will never fully satisfy every member; you're looking for a general thumbs-up, not perfection).

Your list:

-
-
-
-
-
-

2. The Structure: Values, Covenants, and Ground Rules

Values shape the culture of a community. *Covenants* and *ground rules* provide structure to hold the values together, helping members share mutual accountability and hold one another accountable. Covenants are agreements that create trust and foster community. We enter into these relationships based on commitment and mutual acceptance.

Ground rules and covenants are based on love and loyalty and are valid only if all members seek to fulfill the commitments and put their values in practice. In some cases, one party in a relationship may choose to keep a covenant despite the unfaithfulness of the other party (as God often did with Israel, loving them despite their rebellion or rejection).

Not all groups have a written covenant or set of ground rules, but all groups have unwritten values or expectations that are understood by their members. When you develop a written covenant or set of ground rules, you are using the discipline of writing something on paper, which brings more clarity and unity than simply discussing these things.

Keys to Forming Covenants or Ground Rules

1. The values must be generated by the group, not imposed by the leader.
2. The affirmations should always be in the form of "we" statements and must be affirmed by each individual.
3. The covenant should be revisited on a periodic basis so that members remember their commitment to one another.
4. Both logistics and values that support group goals and purposes should be included. For example, here is a very brief list:

   Logistics
   - Where and when we will meet
   - How often we will meet
   - Who is responsible for leading
   - Who will organize meals or snacks
   - What the expectations are for attendance

   Values
   - Accountability
   - Openness
   - Confidentiality
   - Acceptance

5. Covenants or ground rules must be formed over time, through a process that involves everyone.

Check with your ministry leadership about this process. They may already have a tool or some specific values they want every group to embrace.

Process for Creating Ground Rules or a Covenant

The following is a guide for engaging in a healthy process together.

- **Meeting 1:** Ask group members to write two or three values for the group. Define and rank these for your list. Talk about some basic commitments you want to make (when you will meet, how often, and so on).
- **Meeting 2:** Clarify your mission and create a clear statement of why you are meeting (at least for the next six months).

- **Meeting 3:** Clarify your vision. What kind of people do you want to become as you live out your values and complete the mission? (You might want to break into subgroups for some of this process, especially if there are more than six people in the group.)
- **Meeting 4:** Create a working document with all this information on one page. This is not a contract but a statement of unity and commitment. Putting it in writing is a process for clarity, and you can revise it or reshape it as you move ahead. Look at it every six months or so to see if you still affirm it or want to change some things. It is a benchmark for progress, not laws to be obeyed.

A sample covenant appears below, but create your own unique framework for your group.

SAMPLE COVENANT OR GROUND RULES

Leader Sarah Apprentice(s) Kim

1. The mission of our group for this season together is to grow in our ability to serve our local community.
2. We will meet for nine weeks, after which we will evaluate our direction or progress.
3. We will gather from 6:30 pm to 8:00 pm on Tuesdays, and we will arrive on time so we can start and end on time.
4. We will gather at the Johnsons' home for our next season.
5. We will connect with Christ and one another by seeking the presence of Christ daily, and doing a check-in with at least one group member [chosen at each meeting].
6. We will develop and grow by memorizing or meditating on one scripture each month.
7. We will serve the church and the world by identifying a need we all can help meet on a quarterly basis.

Our Vision Is

To become a force for hope and change through love, service, and sacrificial living so we can encourage one another, and to impact our friends and neighbors for Christ.

Our Values Are

- **Openness:** Everyone is given the right to their own opinion, and so-called "dumb questions" are encouraged and respected.
- **Confidentiality:** Anything of a personal nature that is said in the meeting is never repeated outside the meeting without consent. [This is a big trust-builder.]
- **Authenticity:** We will strive to be open and real with one another, respecting opinions and inviting people to share their lives and ideas. We will not judge people but will engage ideas and opinions truthfully.
- **Inclusivity:** We will stay open to new people who can share our mission and values. We will practice together the process for connecting with new people and inviting them to our group.
- **Group Growth:** We will seek to add members and develop leaders as God enables, and we will seek to give life to a new group in which others can experience the community we are enjoying.

Shared Responsibilities

We will share some or all of the following responsibilities: leader, host, prayer coordinator, event planner, administrator, social media coordinator, and service project coordinator.

3. The Strategy: Structures for Growth

Essential Ingredients for Growth in Group Life

All groups share some common objectives for growth. In *Walking the Small Group Tightrope*, Russ Robinson and I name six goals or objectives for a small group, recognizing that leaders will pursue them as they navigate a number of tensions along the way—thus the "tightrope" image of holding something in tension so that the result is balance.[1]

For example, objective #1 below recognizes a truth-life tension. A small group can put all the focus on mastering content or on sharing life stories and ideas. Both are good and essential in a group. However, to pursue spiritual growth, the group must hold truth and life together in a kind of tension, moving back and forth between the two to create harmony and balance.

Whether you are leading a task group, a children's group, an online experience, a home group for adults, or a support group, these six components will frame the context for your small group experience. A group may emphasize some of these components more than others, depending on its focus, but all six should be present in the life of most small groups.

Objective #1: Pursue Spiritual Transformation

Some groups focus only on doctrinal truth and Bible study, while others primarily share needs and concerns. Groups seeking to be transformed into the image of Christ read, study, and speak God's truth *and* apply it to life. Such groups ask, "How will we change or respond to the truth that has been studied and discussed?" As a small group, don't settle for merely gaining information; pursue transformation. When the truth of Scripture sinks into the hearts of members, the opportunity for such transformation exists. So allow the Holy Spirit to work the truth into your hearts to produce lasting change and growth (Romans 12:2).

Objective #2: Practice Intentional Development

As a group, should you concentrate on caregiving or disciple making? The answer is *both*! Groups in which the members help one another grow while also providing care for people in need rarely have attendance problems. When you care for one another, you declare that the church is a family. When you disciple one another for ministry and growth, you are equipping soldiers for the battle. Every leader must face the tension between how much effort to put into caring for people and how much time to spend on developing them. Intentional development occurs when leaders encourage group members to consistently practice both. As Paul says, "Encourage one another and build each other up" (1 Thessalonians 5:11).

Objective #3: Build Authentic Relationships

Groups often struggle to define their relational purpose. They ask, "Do we concentrate on building friendships or do we focus on challenging one another—on accountability?" The answer, again, is *both*. We all want friends—people to laugh and cry with, people to socialize with, people to simply hang out with. But friendship without accountability produces little spiritual growth. Good friends really care about us, challenge our thinking, and remind us to maintain our commitments. Great examples of this dynamic are found between Jonathan and David (1 Samuel 20) and between Jesus and his disciples (John 15:9–17).

Objective #4: Encourage Healthy Conflict

No one enjoys working through conflict. In fact, most of us will do anything to avoid it, hoping the problem will just go away. The real question is how to deal with relational problems in your group without destroying the community you are trying to build. Some in your group might consistently respond with kindness when there is a relational breakdown. They hope that treating the offender nicely—and never naming the offense or pattern of sin—will somehow erase the problem. Others might prefer head-to-head confrontation, eagerly pointing out another person's error and demanding repentance and contrition. But when kindness *and* confrontation are woven together, you will promote reconciliation in your group and create an environment for facing difficult issues with truth and grace (Ephesians 4:25–32).

Objective #5: Enjoy Serving Together

Humility and spiritual growth are fostered when group members unite to serve others. Groups in which members serve together tend to form stronger bonds of community than those that meet only for Bible study and prayer. Something amazing happens when group members serve together in loving relationships: Community is forged while the task is accomplished. Task-focused groups need to create opportunities for community building, while study groups will need to identify ways to serve those outside the group or outside the church.

Objective #6: Create an Inclusive Community

God has called us to love one another (John 13:35) and to reach out to a lost world (Matthew 28:18–20), which requires a group to create intimacy while practicing openness. Remember that there are still many people in your church and outside its walls who need a loving community. If your group hoards what it has or fails to love others as brothers and sisters, it will fail to achieve what God has commanded.

STRATEGY FOR GROUP GROWTH

When small groups weave all six of these objectives into the fabric of the community experience, God seems to pour out his love and blessing on everyone. It's an amazing thing to watch. So use the table below as a tool to jot down at least one idea or strategy for making progress in each area *as a group*. (Your group might not focus on all six of these development themes right now.) Give it a try and see what you can brainstorm.

Purpose to Achieve	Strategy for Group Growth
Spiritual transformation	
Intentional development	
Authentic relationships	
Healthy conflict	
Serving together	
Inclusive community	

TWO KEY FACTORS THAT AFFECT GROWTH

Using the process, structure, and strategy just listed will help you build a spiritual greenhouse in which group members grow into disciples of Christ. However, there are two additional factors that cannot be ignored as you build the greenhouse: *group stages* and *group communication*.

Groups are like families. They move through growth stages and rely on clear, consistent communication to function well over the long haul. Understanding these stages and communication patterns will make you aware of the shifting dynamics of group life.

Group Stages

Leaders often take the blame for changes in group dynamics that are, in reality, simply the result of a shift to a new stage of the group's natural life cycle. Groups, like all living organisms, move through stages of development. The table on page 84 can help you take a snapshot of your group and plan a strategy for moving productively through each stage. As you and your group move through these stages, be sure to talk about what is happening, what folks are feeling, what changes can be made—and then agree to work together on them.

Forming Stage

New groups gather and the members begin to connect and get to know one another. Generally, this is a positive "honeymoon stage" for a group.

Norming Stage

The group members discuss or naturally practice ground rules (covenant), set expectations, define mission or goals, and "do group" together. They begin to gel and gain clarity as a group while deepening relationships.

Storming Stage

This is a crucial stage for the group. Some experts refer to this period as "transition," and often a group will arrive at this place more than once over its life cycle. The honeymoon is over. People begin to express differences of opinion and wonder about other members. They might have some minor conflicts or dissatisfaction, long to go deeper, or need to name reality about their feelings. Here a group decides to either (1) be a real community by entering the chaos, owning the process, accepting one another's flaws and quirks, loving one another, and getting to work; or (2) stay stuck by withdrawing into pseudo-community, pretending all is well, never really sharing deeply, and just going through the routines of group life but never growing beyond basic head knowledge.

Performing Stage

Here the group rolls up its sleeves and gets to work. Some experts refer to this as the "work" or "action" phase of a group. People are on mission and engaging relationally, speaking the truth in love, working out differences and disagreements, growing in love for God and others, and making progress in line with the vision and values they created earlier.

Reproduction Stage

Some groups develop an apprentice leader or two, add people, and eventually form a second group. They may simply bring in new potential leaders, train them, and send them out to start new groups.

Termination Stage

Either by design or by simple recognition of reality, most groups will come to an end. Processing an ending is very important. *DO NOT NEGLECT THIS!* Celebrate the good things,

HELPING GROUP MEMBERS PROCESS GROWING PAINS

	Core Stages				Other Stages	
Stage	**Forming**	**Norming**	**Storming**	**Performing**	**Reproduction**	**Termination**
Average Number of Meetings per Stage	3-5	4-6	4-5	10-20	6-8	2-4
Members' Questions	Who is in the group? Do I like my group?	Do I fit here? How is our group doing? Are we becoming a community?	Are we really open with each other? Will this group accomplish its mission?	How will we do this? What can we accomplish together? Will we take the risk?	Will we survive? How will we change?	Did we grow? What did we learn? Will I join another group?
Members' Feelings	Excited Expectant Awkward	Comfortable Relaxed Open	Tense Anxious Impatient Doubtful	Eager Open Vulnerable Supportive	Grieved Enthusiastic Mournful Expectant Afraid	Respectful Reflective Thankful Sad
Members' Role	Gather information about others	Give information Accept others	Provide feedback Express frustration	Express feelings Use my gifts Take ownership Accept challenges	Express concerns Accept reality Discuss changes Give blessing	Show love Express thanks Affirm relationships
Leader's Response	Caring Clear Accepting	Affirm Give feedback Exude warmth Model Christ-likeness	Confront Encourage Challenge	Challenge Affirm Guide Release	Listen actively Acknowledge feelings Affirm members	Review Reflect Respond
Leader's Role	Communicate vision Promote sharing Define goals	Generate trust Discuss values Facilitate relationships Create covenant	Practice self-disclosure Reexamine covenant Be flexible	Provide service opportunities Clarify goals Begin seeking second apprentice Celebrate results	Cast vision Pray for launch Create subgroups Communicate with apprentice	Celebrate Give gifts Celebrate communion Bring closure

the growth, the stories, and the joy. Grieve any losses or disappointments. Agree to learn from this experience, even if the group was hard for people, or not great for them, or just did not work out as a whole. It's okay. Try again to launch another group, or encourage people to try another kind of group. Don't just stop meeting. Have a final meeting so there is closure. You are going to see most of these people again, maybe every week at church, and you want to end well, without hurt feelings or unresolved issues.

REFLECTION

Stages

If you are currently leading a small group, what stage is it in at this time?

What indicators lead you to believe that your group is in this stage of development?

How are you preparing for the next stage? What needs to happen before you transition into the next stage of development?

Group Communication

Communication is essential to developing healthy relationships, healthy families, and healthy churches. Communication is also essential in small groups. Without proper communication with God and with others, your group will become stagnant and superficial. The following four channels of communication (adapted from Ralph Neighbour, *Where Do We Go from Here?*) characterize the levels of interaction in a small group.

1. God to Group

Your group members want to hear from God. They seek his will and desire to hear his voice. So take time in your group to be silent and to read the Scriptures. Listen as the Holy Spirit works through the Word of God to convict you and challenge you. Listen for the still, small voice of the Lord as he communicates his purpose for your group or for a particular meeting through the Spirit, through others, and through his Word.

2. Group to God

Your group members should not only hear from God but also respond to him. A response can take the form of a prayer, an expression of praise, a reading of Scripture back to God, a song, or a quiet devotion that communicates their feelings to God.

3. Group Member to Group Member

Vulnerable, authentic, truthful communication among group members will enable them to become a powerful vehicle for life change. Groups grow when members express feelings, words of encouragement, or hurts to one another. Jesus said, "You will know the truth, and the truth will set you free" (John 8:32). Groups characterized by truth-telling are groups that experience freedom in Christ. Groups avoid becoming superficial and pretentious when members speak loving, caring truths to one another.

4. Group to World

It is the responsibility of believers in Christ to take the message of Christianity to a lost and dying world. As a small group, you proclaim the truth as you have opportunity to speak with people who might not yet be connected to God. You proclaim the truth both verbally and through your deeds. Reflect on how your group will take action to deliver the message of Christianity to your community and to the world.

SPIRITUAL PRACTICES FOR BUILDING COMMUNITY IN GROUPS

Diana Shiflett, in her book *Spiritual Practices in Community* (see the Addional Resources section at the end of this chapter for information), invites believers in Christ into fresh experiences *in* community and into spiritual practices *as* a small group community. I have taken the liberty to highlight eight of the ten practices she covers in her book and have summarized the examples here. As she affirms, these can be done in all kinds of groups, from boardrooms to dinner tables and beyond.

Practice #1: Two Minutes of Silence

Purpose: To quiet the group and open space for God.

How-to: Say to the group, "Let's sit in silence for two minutes and simply become aware of God's presence." Then end with, "What did you notice?"

Practice #2: Breath Prayer

Purpose: To slow down, center on God, and pray with the body.

How-to: Invite each person to choose a short phrase (e.g., "Lord, I am yours"). Have them breathe in the first half of the phrase and out for the second half. Do this for one to two minutes. This practices offers a rich, smooth rhythm for prayer.

Practice #3: *Lectio Divina* (Scripture Listening)

Purpose: To hear Scripture as personal invitation, not information.

How-to: Read a short passage three times. Have the group simply listen with eyes closed the first time. Then, after the second reading, ask, "What word or phrase stood out? What do you sense God saying?" Read the passage a third time, and then ask, "What is God inviting you to do?"

Practice #4: Imaginative Scripture Prayer

Purpose: To meet Jesus in a story from Scripture using "sanctified imagination."

How-to: Select a passage from the Gospels that contains a story or teaching environment around Jesus. Read the Gospel scene slowly and invite the group members to imagine themselves in it, picturing the setting and paying attention to thoughts, sights, sounds, smells they might experience if they were with Jesus in that space. Then ask them to share what they saw, heard, or felt.

Practice #5: The *Examen* (Group Reflection)

Purpose: To notice God's presence in daily life as the group reflects on the day.

How-to: Guide your group by discussing the following questions:

- Where did you experience God's presence today?
- Where did you resist or feel distant from God?
- What might the Holy Spirit be focusing on for you?

Practice #6: Story Sharing (Life Snapshot)

Purpose: To build trust and deeper connection as the members share stories.
How-to: Give two to three minutes for each person in the group to share a moment from their week. Ask the listeners to respond only with gratitude or encouragement—no fixing, giving advice, or sharing their own story instead of listening.

Practice #7: Confession and Release

Note: This is a practice only for groups with high trust among members.

Purpose: To practice honest vulnerability and humble forgiveness.
How-to: Introduce a sentence starter such as, "God, I confess that . . ." The group will follow this with a few moments of silence and then close with a communal prayer of forgiveness—for example, "Lord have mercy and forgive us."

Practice #8: Group Discernment (Listening Before Decisions)

Purpose: To hear God about a decision or direction a group member is considering.
How-to: Introduce this practice by engaging in one minute of silence, and then go around the group and ask each person to express any sense, scripture, or nudge they perceived. Don't allow any debates or challenges until after the listening round. Just stay with, "I am hearing," "I wonder who would be a good person to share this with," and similar comments.

ADDITIONAL RESOURCES

Henry Cloud and John Townsend, *Making Small Groups Work* (Zondervan, 2003). Great for creating ground rules, for understanding the group process, and for knowing the role of the leader in guiding groups to become safe and authentic.

Todd Hunter, *Christianity Beyond Belief* (InterVarsity, 2010). Hunter provides a very engaging look into the life of discipleship. He states, "You know that if you die tonight you'll go to heaven, but what if you knew you were going to *live* tomorrow?" He calls on believers in Christ to reframe their salvation to focus on *life* instead of just heaven and hell.

Jenn Miller and Tara Peppers, *Finding the Flow* (InterVarsity, 2008). This book focuses on how to be guided by the Holy Spirit as you lead a group and provides spiritual and relational exercises that a group can do together.

Bill Search, *Simple Small Groups* (Baker, 2008). Bill helps group leaders focus on the core of what small groups are all about while avoiding the many distractions that take leaders off course and make group life more complex and cluttered than God intended.

Diana Shifflett, *Spiritual Practices in Community* (InterVarsity, 2018). This resource invites your group to enter the beautiful and sacred space of community while enhancing that experience by sharing transforming practices as a group. I highly recommend this book for groups, retreats, and in extended devotional settings.

Note

1. Bill Donahue and Russ Robinson, *Walking the Small Group Tightrope* (Zondervan, 2003).

CHAPTER 6

LEADING LIFE-CHANGING MEETINGS

Small group meetings can be exciting or frustrating—often at the same time! The possibilities are endless when you consider all the personalities and dynamics represented in a group. Whether you experience chaos or community may depend on any number of factors. You cannot control everything, but there are many things you can do to invite the Holy Spirit to work in a powerful way among your people in a meeting.

In this chapter, I will help you prepare for a meeting and understand the various group dynamics that are involved. There are a number of skills you'll need for leading a group effectively, but don't feel overwhelmed, as you won't have to master them all right away. I have also included some materials to help you put these leadership skills into practice. Finally, I have included some tools you can use to evaluate your group and your leadership, which will provide you with the feedback you need along the way. So get ready to turn small group meetings into exciting moments in which you witness Christ at work as he builds his church.

LEADING ONLINE GROUPS

Before we proceed, we need to recognize the obstacles and opportunities presented by *online groups*. These types of groups have emerged in church ministries and became prevalent especially during and after the COVID-19 pandemic. You will need to exercise wisdom and discernment if you are building and leading such a group. Here is a short list of things to consider and to be wary about when it comes to leading online groups.

Opportunities for Online Groups

- **Lower Barriers to entry:** People who can't attend in person (due to childcare, mobility issues, time constraints) can participate onscreen in a hybrid form of group.
- **Broader reach:** Groups can include people from multiple campuses, cities, or countries.
- **Flexible scheduling:** Shorter, more frequent meetings become possible.
- **Increased accessibility:** Introverts may feel more comfortable sharing online than in a living room or other face-to-face settings.
- **Easier resource integration:** Screen sharing for Bible passages, videos, documents, and prayer prompts is easier and familiar. Also, use of chat features can allow people to capture ideas without interrupting the conversation.

Obstacles for Online Groups

- **Digital fatigue:** Many companies and organizations now employ digital platforms for their meetings. This means participants arrive tired from working on screens and have a dwindling desire to continue this format when their group gathers.

- **Technical barriers:** Wi-Fi issues, poor audio/video reception, unfamiliar digital meeting tools, and other technical issues can disrupt the flow of the meeting.
- **Limited nonverbal cues:** Facial expressions, body language, and side conversations are harder to discern. In addition, people may bring practices or habits from work into the small group culture (such as frequently moving on and off screen during the meeting, turning off the camera, shooting humorous texts to one another, and the like).
- **Relational distance:** Participants may feel less connected to one another, less willing to share, and hesitant to "interrupt" or speak up when they have questions. In addition, there is the reality of participants joining from various time zones.
- **Attention drift:** Notifications, unwanted engagement from third parties, multitasking, plus all the distractions that come from a home environment (pets, small children requiring attention, typical bustle of family life, and the like) can pull people away from the focus of a conversation.

Best Practices for Online Groups

- **Technology:** Test links, audio, waiting rooms, and breakout rooms before the meeting.
- **Intentionality:** Emotional tone in online settings can shift quickly. Silence feels longer and interruptions feel sharper, so be intentional as you lead.
- **Presence:** You have to work a bit harder to cultivate presence in online meetings. Make eye contact, call people by name, and be warm and friendly.
- **Distractions:** Plan on the fact that people will be more distracted in digital meetings. Use activities and interaction, not long monologues.
- **Group size:** Seven to ten participants is ideal; beyond that, group discussions become difficult and participation can begin to drop.

Tips for Leading Discussions

- Start with easy, relational statements to warm people up: "It's great to see everyone joining. In a minute, I will ask you to share something good from your week."
- Use names intentionally: "Okay . . . Alex, what would you like to share?"
- Limit the teaching segments to twenty minutes. Consider taking a break after ten minutes to have the group members write down what they have learned so far or to get in pairs to discuss. This breaks up the teaching time and keeps energy up.
- Encourage everyone's camera to be on, but don't mandate it.
- Create an environment where people *want* to show up fully. Be friendly, accessible, notice the group members, and seek to include everyone in the discussion.
- Use features like chat, polls, or breakout rooms. This increases interaction.

- Use structured turn-taking: "Let's hear from two more people. Who'd like to go next?"
- Embrace silence. Give people space to think before moving on.

How to Help People Feel Connected

- Open the room five minutes early for informal connection and catching up.
- Greet each person by name as they join the meeting.
- Begin with a "connection round" where everyone shares briefly.
- Show empathy visibly—nod, smile, affirm, listen. Notice one another and reply.
- Create rituals: Use the same opening question, prayer rhythm, or check-in for each meeting to create structure for the group.
- Follow up individually with texts or messages after meaningful conversations.
- Celebrate birthdays, milestones, and answered prayers. Yes, these kinds of celebrations can happen even in a virtual room.

Sample Online Meeting Plan and Structure (75–85 minutes)

- **5 minutes:** Welcome and relational connection time
- **20 minutes:** Scripture/video/teaching (with a short break after 10 minutes)
- **30 to 40 minutes:** Discussion and breakout interaction
- **15 minutes:** Prayer and next steps
- **5 minutes:** Informal after-meeting hang for those who want to connect further

PREPARATION FOR TYPICAL IN-PERSON MEETINGS

Whether you are meeting in person or online, focused work on meeting preparation and planning will make your group much more effective and successful. Preparation accomplishes three things:

1. It communicates to members you have a sense of direction and leadership.
2. It gives the group confidence in your overall leadership.
3. It allows you to alter the course of a meeting (if necessary) because you can make choices regarding what issues you will cover during it.

Setting the Stage for an Effective Meeting

(Note that there may be variations with online groups.)

- Carefully think through the Meeting Planner worksheet (see page 98).
- Make sure everyone knows where and when the meeting will take place.

- If you have a meeting host, contact them about details for the meeting. The host should create a warm, caring atmosphere; make sure the logistics (refreshments, seating, and so on) have been accounted for; and greet people as they enter the room or online space.

Designing an Effective Meeting

Russ Robinson, a ministry partner and friend, uses four key questions or themes to organize the content of a meeting. This "Head, Hands, Heart, and Homework" approach will help you shape the discussion and action components of a meeting, serve as a guide for the entire meeting, and especially aid you in how you use the Bible. Here are the four questions:

1. **Head:** What do you want group members to know or understand?
2. **Heart:** What do you hope group members will feel or experience?
3. **Hands:** What are you going to do together with what you learn?
4. **Homework:** What is the "assignment" for activity, next steps, or relationships between meetings?

DESIRED OUTCOME

Head ***What do I want group members to know or understand?*** The list of spiritual gifts in Romans 12; 1 Corinthians 12; Ephesians 4	**Heart** ***What do I hope group members will feel or experience?*** Prized by God and each other for their uniqueness
Hands ***What are we going to do together with what we know?*** The spiritual gifts assessment in the *Network Series**	**Homework** ***What is the assignment for activity or relationships between meetings?*** How they expect to begin using their gifts

* See the Additional Resources section in chapter 3 for details on this resource.

CREATING A MEETING PLAN

Now that you have thought through the "Head, Heart, Hands, and Homework" framework, it's time to create a plan for the meeting. On the following pages, you will find two tools to help you structure your next meeting: the Meeting Planner and the Meeting Preparation Checklist.

The Meeting Planner

The Meeting Planner (see page 98) will help you think through the overall purpose of your group. This planner is a tool to help frame your meeting.

Notice that in the Sample Meeting Planner (see page 99), there's a five-minute gap from 7:25–7:30. This little extra space allows you to shift focus, get something to eat, prepare the "room" if you are broadcasting online, update latecomers, and move into another space (for example, from the kitchen into the living room for in-person meetings or to the breakout rooms for online meetings). There is also a twenty- to twenty-five minute time built into the end of the meeting for personal conversations and having that "meeting after the meeting" that often happens. In online settings, you might want to use this time to do a follow-up call (either by switching to Facetime, a phone, or staying in the online meeting) and to have some chat time.

Note this is a *framework* for planning your meeting time, not a rigid guideline. For example, imagine that a member arrives and—even though it's their birthday this week—they tell the group they have been having real problems with an employee and had to fire that person today. The member feels awful and almost did not come at all. In this instance, you will want to adjust your schedule to support that group member. In other cases, the Bible discussion might go deeper than expected, with some members opening their hearts to God's work, and you want to have the flexibility in your schedule to allow that to take place.

Always remember that the *Holy Spirit* is the official leader of the group. The curriculum, experiences, activities, agenda, and your leadership—*especially* your leadership—are tools in his hands. By having a framework or agenda, you know what to say yes to and what to say no to, what to add or to drop, what is urgent to cover in the current meeting and what can be delayed to the next meeting, and what can be handled offline or between meetings.

The Meeting Preparation Checklist

The Meeting Preparation Checklist (see page 101) is a tool to prompt your thinking and help you remember details. The checklist uses the acronym PLAN, which stands for:

- **P**urpose of the meeting
- **L**ogistics to be managed
- **A**ctivities and work to be done
- **N**eeds of members and others

Once you use the checklist a few times, you will be able to prepare for in-person or online meetings with confidence and creativity. The checklist is fairly self-explanatory. If you have questions on how to use it or how it applies to your particular kind of group or ministry, consult your coach or ministry leaders.

CHOOSING THE RIGHT MATERIAL FOR YOUR GROUP

Choosing the right study or discussion material/curriculum for your group can be challenging considering the number of options now found in bookstores and online. The Choosing a Curriculum Flowchart (see page xx) has been designed to help you sift through the myriad of materials to find something your group needs.

A Few Tips About Curriculum

Curriculum Is a Tool

Whatever material you choose, it should never lead the group. It can provide a helpful role or focus, but remember that the group leader(s) is ultimately the guide. Don't forfeit opportunities for extended prayer or service, or cut short a necessary community-building activity, because "we have to get through the curriculum." Jesus did not say, "Go therefore into all the world and complete the curriculum!" Your goal is ultimately to make disciples—Christ followers—who are obedient to Jesus, yielded to the Spirit, and loving toward others.

Curriculum Is Not Intended as a Substitute for the Bible

As just stated, curriculum is a *tool.* Study guides and other materials should be used to enhance the group's purpose and move people toward biblical truth.

Don't Feel Obligated to Finish All the Questions

Good leaders know what questions to use and how many of them to discuss. If there are too many questions provided in the curriculum you've chosen, choose a few good ones (five to seven at most). Most times, a few good questions followed by the right kind of process

MEETING PLANNER

Date: ________	Details	Who's Responsible	Time	Comments or Issues
Purpose				
Logistics				
Activities				
Needs				

SAMPLE MEETING PLANNER

Date: January 11	Details	Who's Responsible	Time	Comments or Issues
Purpose (Head, Heart, Hands, Homework)	To help members understand spiritual gifts and why they are needed.	Kim and I will discuss this on the phone.		Encourage people to take assessment and GIFTS class; pray each day for Spirit to empower us; know gifts of others.
Logistics	Meet at Kim's; cake for Kevin's birthday	Cake: Mike and Sandy Kim: email reminder		Ask everyone to write a note for Kevin.
Activities	1. Birthday & notes 2. Life story—Mike 3. Break 4. Bible—I Corinthians 5. Prayer—gifts/needs 6. End then move to personal time/updates ** Discuss new curriculum	1. Kim to Lead 2. Mike 3. N/A 4. Me and Kim 5. Kim to lead 6. Me and Kim ** Me: curriculum	7:00-7:15 7:15-7:25 7:25-7:30 7:30-8:00 8:00-8:20 8:20-8:45 8:45-9:00	1. Everyone will read their note. 4. Determine who handles what questions. 5. Focus is on gifts, then shift to personal needs and community. 6. Check in with members. ** Hand out copies of new study guide to prep for next week.
Needs	The Harrises are still looking for work.	Group prayer		Update this based on prayer time and personal connections at the end of meeting.

will be more than enough for your group—it's better to have a great discussion while grappling with a few questions than to answer all of them at a superficial level. The goal is to engage people with the truth of God's Word as it relates to their own heart and growth. (The exception might be for groups that are designed for learning certain truths and mastering some level of content.)

Make Sure the Material Used Is Group Friendly

Many small group studies are designed for understanding Bible content, not for building relationships or generating a deep sense of community and caring. Look closely at not only the questions but also the process. Does the curriculum allow for lots of interaction? Does it ask personal disclosure questions that challenge people to open up and share their lives? Or is it filled with content-based "what" questions, often ignoring personal "why" or "how" questions?

Look for Engaging Application Questions

An application question that simply asks, "How would this apply to your life?" is weak. You want a question that asks something like this: "It's clear from this passage that we need to share our faith with others, and it is clear that we all know how and that it would please God, but let's talk about why it is so hard for you and me to start spiritual conversations with seekers. Are there fears or other barriers you face in communicating the gospel? How does it feel when you picture yourself talking to an unsaved person about Christ?" These kinds of questions will probe your group members' motives, thoughts, feelings, and needs. Only then can they truly encourage and pray for one another.

Key Questions When Choosing Curriculum/Material

Note: Your church may already provide material or allow leaders and groups to choose from a few approved options. Check in with your church staff.

What Is Our Purpose?

The curriculum should support the purpose of the group. This purpose may change as the group moves through seasons of growth, maturity, and experience. If a group starts as grief support for those who have lost loved ones, the curriculum should reflect that purpose. As people move through the stages of grief, a leader may see that the group members need to understand more about God. As a result, a curriculum on the attributes of God may then be appropriate.

MEETING PREPARATION CHECKLIST (PLAN)

Purpose

What will the meeting accomplish?

- ❒ Write out "Head, Heart, Hands, Homework" objectives.
- ❒ Write out the meeting agenda on meeting planner.
- ❒ ______________________________
- ❒ ______________________________

Logistics

Are the details for the meeting prepared?

- ❒ Seating, lighting, temperature, online setup factors
- ❒ Distractions eliminated (phones, noise, people)
- ❒ Refreshments
- ❒ Music playing during arrival
- ❒ Childcare arrangements
- ❒ Location set for future meeting(s)
- ❒ ______________________________
- ❒ ______________________________

Activities

What is the agenda and work to be done?

- ❒ Discussion starter, social mixer
- ❒ Group prayer and worship (singing for some groups)
- ❒ Social time or structured exercise/project (materials needed)
- ❒ Bible engagement time
- ❒ Updates to be made
- ❒ ______________________________
- ❒ ______________________________

Needs

What are our concerns for members or others?

- ❒ Unresolved relational problems
- ❒ Financial needs
- ❒ Tough decisions to make
- ❒ Health concerns
- ❒ Family issues
- ❒ ______________________________
- ❒ ______________________________

Where Is the Group Spiritually?

It is wise to take the spiritual pulse of your group to determine the level of curriculum appropriate for it. If the group is dominated by people investigating the claims of Christ, make sure the questions are appropriate for them. Listen without making rash judgments, don't appear to have all the answers, and deal with the issues facing them as explorers of the faith. Allow them to process information, ask hard questions, and raise objections. Use a Bible version that is easy for them to read and use. (*The Journey NIV* from Zondervan, designed with questions and insights for spiritual seekers, is a great Bible for this kind of group.)

New and growing believers can handle more difficult Bible discussions and are more willing to tolerate religious jargon. Even so, try to avoid using a lot of religious terminology. Believers who have been around the church longer may feel comfortable with terms like *redemption* or *justification*, but avoid using them too much with newer Christ followers unless you expect to spend the time to adequately explain what those terms mean.

What Are the Group's Key Needs?

This question relates to the purpose question, but it allows a group to address real needs and still accomplish what is its overall purpose. For example, couples in a group may desire growth in their marriage relationships. Their group may actually be a serving group designed to help meet needs at a local homeless shelter. In this case, as couples they could meet for thirty minutes prior to serving together for a brief study and discussion about marital issues.

What Is the Group's Current Focus?

Sometimes leaders choose material focused on immediate needs but fail to consider the long-range vision for their group. For instance, your group may be completing a study on Christianity in the workplace, and now some in the group want to study the book of Galatians. The question for you to ask is *why*. How does studying Galatians fit with the overall group direction for the coming year? Are there elements in that book of the Bible that would be appropriate to focus on, or would it be better to study it when it makes more sense in the life cycle of the group?

Try to provide a flow for the group unless the situation dictates an abrupt change in focus. For example, suppose your small group is completing a personal growth curriculum. Now might be the appropriate time for you to identify one of the areas covered in that book and do an extended series or study on it. A section on finances, for instance, could be expanded to deal with using finances in a compassionate way to help the poor. That would be a great step toward casting a vision for serving others and would not appear to be an abrupt curriculum change.

CHOOSING A CURRICULUM FLOWCHART

What Is Our Purpose?
- Bible knowledge
- Spiritual disciplines
- Strong relationships
- Caregiving
- Processing life's issues

Where Is the Group Spiritually?
- Seekers
- New believers
- Maturing believers
- Mixed

What Are Our Key Needs?
- Discipleship
- Encouragement
- Obedience
- Marriage enrichment
- Knowledge

What Is Our Current Focus?
- Issues between men and women
- Workplace
- Marriage
- Understanding Scripture
- Relationship building

What Are Our Limitations?
- Time
- Location
- Size of group
- Duration of group

What Is the Best Curriculum?
- Scripture passage
- Topic centered/issue centered
- Book of the Bible
- Church-provided study
- Book with study guide
- Curriculum series
- Sermon-based study

What Are the Group's Limitations?

Don't waste your time looking at curriculum designed for a two-hour study when your group has only forty minutes to meet. Make sure to consider the time, location (are you in a distracting environment, whether in person or online?), and size of your group (four people can deal with more questions than nine, assuming you want to allow everyone to participate).

Note that ten people in an online group may be in ten different environments, assuming each member is in a unique space. This may be a strength or challenge, but be prepared. For example, one member might have two dogs and a toddler in a home, another might be calling in from an office in Europe because they are traveling, and maybe someone else is sitting on a deck with a sunrise in the background. This may or may not affect how you use the material and whether there should be "homework" or reading done ahead of time so everyone is in sync, regardless of their individual setting.

What Is the Best Curriculum?

Many churches today use sermon-based or church-produced materials for small group content. There are also streaming options and online publishing organizations that produce materials for use by small groups. In many churches, if they have confidence in their group leaders, they will allow those leaders to choose the materials (usually after approval by the staff leadership).

Regardless of the materials being used, the curriculum should be your *servant*, not your *master*. Use it to help people grow. Regularly evaluate and adjust your expectations. Set it aside if it gets in the way of engagement and growth of members. If you focus on integrating biblical truths with life development, you won't even be disappointed. Regardless of your approach—Bible study, topical, or sermon questions—you won't go wrong if you connect truth with life. Also, if applicable, remember to stay in communication with your church staff person as you make or propose changes to the materials you want to use. This is a team effort.

One last note on choosing your curriculum. If you use AI for content research and study material development, make sure you are not creating group materials in a vacuum. Again, engage your staff at the church about AI and any policies or guidelines they have in place.

GROUP DYNAMICS

When you are conducting a meeting, it's important to always be aware of the dynamics of a group. This requires paying attention to the kinds of roles people are playing, whether they are engaged or not, their individual learning styles and personalities, and their spiritual gifts. The interaction of these factors makes each group unique.

Group Roles

Often members take on certain roles—sometimes consciously and sometimes without really knowing they are doing it. People will also take on different roles at different stages of your group. Below are some supportive and destructive group roles you might want to be aware of.

Supportive Roles

Note: You are not trying to judge or "peg" someone into a role. You simply want to be aware that people can take on a "personality" or way of engaging conversations when they are in a group. Be aware of patterns and habits as you facilitate learning and discussions.

- **Information Seeker:** Asks other members to tell more of their story.
- **Opinion Seeker:** Takes an active interest in what other members are thinking.
- **Initiator:** Offers new ideas and new ways of doing things. Often sets the pace in a discussion.
- **Elaborator:** Wants more than just the facts in a story. Adds color to the discussion.
- **Tension Reliever:** Often uses gentle humor to relieve tense situations. Identifies with a person in the group and seeks to connect with their feelings: "Sounds like this is hard. I have felt that way myself."
- **Reviewer:** Tends to provide summary statements and clarity statements.
- **Consensus Seeker:** Looks to see what the group is thinking and whether there is agreement on issues or decisions.
- **Encourager:** Finds ways to build up others in the group.
- **Standard Bearer:** Guards the values of the group and defends them, keeping them central and clear.

Destructive Roles

- **Aggressor:** Insults and criticizes others. May show strong jealousy.
- **Rabbit Chaser:** Consistently focuses on stories or issues irrelevant to the topic at hand but very exciting to them.
- **Recognition Seeker:** Focuses primarily on their own achievements or successes.
- **Dominator:** Monopolizes group interaction. Tries to control discussions.
- **Special-Interest Advocate:** Focuses on personal pet peeves or areas of interest despite the topic being discussed or the direction of discussion.
- **Negativist:** Might be a perfectionist who is never satisfied with anything. Quick to point out the downside of any issue or topic.
- **Detailer:** Focuses too much on minutia. Often loses the forest for the sake of the trees.
- **Practical Joker:** Distracts people with jokes and comments rather than using humor positively. This is often a defense mechanism for the person and is used whenever a discussion gets too personal.

Your Role as Leader

Your job as a leader is not to peg each person in order to figure out what their role is. Roles may change from time to time; you simply need to be aware that these kinds of personal styles exist in a group. Listen with a sensitive spirit and heart to each person. Ask probing questions that help get behind each role. If you have problems working with a particular type of person, consult your coach or ministry leaders for ways to solve the problem and deal with the relationship.

Learning Styles

Educators and trainers of adults often refer to certain "learning styles." Three major types are visual learners, auditory learners, kinesthetic learners. Effective leaders use a variety of presentation and discussion techniques to communicate effectively to each kind of learner.

Visual Learners

Visual learners respond well to charts, diagrams, and other visual stimuli. They like handouts and enjoy parables and stories. They are visual thinkers—that is, they respond well to word pictures and vivid, descriptive stories that allow them to picture what is happening.

Tips for the leader: Use handouts, newspaper articles, storyboards, digital images, paper and crayons, and objects to keep the attention of your visual learners.

Auditory Learners

Auditory learners enjoy learning by hearing. They would rather engage in a discussion on an issue than read a book about it. Some of them may be avid readers, but in general they would rather listen to a story than read one.

Tips for the leader: Use subgroups to allow all members to participate in discussions. Allow members to respond verbally to questions and decisions. Use background music during prayer times or at the beginning of the meeting. Consider breakout rooms for online settings.

Kinesthetic Learners

These folks like to touch and feel things and participate in the action. They learn by doing. While a visual learner might be motivated to help someone in need by seeing a picture of that person in a news feed, the kinesthetic learner might be motivated by a field trip to an inner city.

Tips for the leader: Utilize objects and experiences for your group. Plan outings and events that allow members to experience truth in action. Allow kinesthetic learners to learn by trial and error rather than by simply telling them the answers.

Personalities: God Made Us All Different!

My purpose here is not to help you identify each person's personality in some technical sense. Rather, I want you to understand that the people in your group are wired differently.

Again, do not spend a lot of time trying to peg each person in your group to a particular personality type. Simply be aware of the tendencies of each personality that might be in your group.

Below is a series of questions you might ask as you think of each group member.

- Do they tend to be more introverted or more extroverted? Does extensive interaction with people tend to energize them (extroverted) or drain them (introverted)?
- Do they experience life with their senses or more intuitively? Do they make insightful judgments about the way life is and how it functions, or do they tend to seek experiences in which they can taste, touch, see, smell, and hear what is happening around them?
- Do they initially process information and decisions with their head or with their heart? Are they more logical and cognitive in nature (head), or are they "feelers" who tend to respond more emotionally (heart)?
- Do they approach life in a structured or unstructured fashion? That is, are they more likely to plan out each day of a family vacation before they leave the house or are they more likely to rent a car and decide along the way?

Helping Members Use Their Spiritual Gifts

Here is a process for helping people deploy their spiritual gifts in your small group. If you follow this process, it will help your group function more effectively and allow each member to grow and mature in their area of giftedness.

1. *Cast a vision for mutual ministry*. Together, read and study Ephesians 4:11–13 and 1 Corinthians 14:26. Help your group understand the value of serving others together and serving one another.
2. *Help members identify their gifts*. Encourage members to use spiritual gift assessment tools (such as in the *Network Series*) or classes offered by the church.
3. *Discuss each person's giftedness*. Ask members to explain their gifts to the group and how they might use them to encourage other members.
4. *Serve in areas of giftedness*. Allow people in your small group to serve according to areas of giftedness and passions.
5. *Consider ministry opportunities*. Discuss ministry opportunities, outside the group, that will utilize people's giftedness.

The Role of the Holy Spirit in Group Dynamics

We have already stated that the Holy Spirit gifts each member of the group so the group functions as a body. However, he works in many other ways. He guides people and teaches them from the Word. He can also work through promptings and experiences. As a group leader, be sensitive to the working of the Holy Spirit as he moves among group members. Here are a few suggestions that will help you be open and sensitive to his leading.

- Pray that the Holy Spirit would do his work of conviction and teaching during your group meeting.
- Be sensitive to group consensus. If the members sense that there should be a change in direction, this may be the voice of the Spirit. Don't automatically assume that your agenda is the only spiritual agenda.
- If you sense a strong conviction from the Spirit of God to discuss a certain matter or issue, feel free to tell this to the group. Don't force them to agree with you; simply explain that you sense God wants you to share some feelings or issues. Then allow the group and the Word of God to guide you as you move forward.
- Allow time for the Holy Spirit to work. Sometimes it's best to wait if there is no consensus on an issue. Ask members to pray and to seek the will of God. Allow God's Spirit to work within people over time.

Remember, the Holy Spirit wants to edify and unite your group. This does not mean all members will agree on all issues, but it does mean they should be willing to submit to one another as they seek consensus, understanding this consensus is likely the result of the Spirit of God working among them to develop community and mutuality. In all cases, verify promptings of the Spirit through the teaching of the Bible. Where the Word of God is clear, obey. Where the Scriptures are silent, seek the will of God and group consensus as each person submits their agenda to Christ and is willing to compromise for the sake of the group.

SKILLS

Discussion Starters and Group Connectors

Using group openers is a basic yet essential small group skill. Icebreaker ideas and "share questions" are designed to facilitate discussion about the members' personal lives and help them open up more freely. They are not designed for simple yes or no answers.

Use discretion with these questions and statements. Some will evoke deep and serious responses. Others are light and funny. If your group is new, use questions and icebreakers that focus on information about people's lives (where they grew up, where they went to school, how they came to your church, where they work, what they think about certain events in our culture, and so on). As intimacy develops in your group, begin to challenge people with more in-depth questions that evoke feelings, thoughts, and insights. (In online settings, this would be a good place to use breakout rooms.)

DISCUSSION STARTERS

Here are questions the members can answer about themselves:

"What is your favorite movie? Why?"

"If money were no problem and you could choose one place in the world to travel to for a week, what would that place be? Why?"

"What are your two most favorite summer activities? Why are they your favorites?" (You can even have them pair off and share these activities with one another.)

"Who is your number one advisor in life? Why?"

"What is one of your biggest pet peeves?"

"What might people be surprised to find out that you can do?"

"You have three wishes. What would you wish for?"

"If you suddenly lost your eyesight, what one thing would you miss seeing the most?"

"What is a daring thing you have done? What made it so daring?"

"What are you willing to admit is your favorite way to waste time?"

"You have one minute to speak to the entire nation on television. What one or two key things would you like to tell the people of your country?"

"What's the story behind the longest time you've gone without sleep?"

"What were the circumstances surrounding your first date?"

"Who is the most famous person you've known or met? How did it happen?"

"If you could do one miracle (other than make the whole world Christian), what would you do? Why?"

"What do you miss most about childhood?"

"What is your biggest fear about death?"

"If you could go to college (or go to college again), what would you study?"

"What's the worst storm or disaster you've been in? What was it like?"

continued on the next page

"What was the most boring day, event, or period of time you can remember?"

"What day of your life would you most like to relive? Why?"

"What's the smallest space you've lived in? What was it like?"

"In high school, what did (or would have) your classmates voted you when it came to 'most likely to ________________________________'?"

"Just for the fun or thrill of it, what would you like to do before you die?"

"What would your number two career choice be?"

"If you were a time traveler, what period would you most like to visit? Why?"

"What was one of the greatest adventures you have ever been on?"

"If you could invent a gadget to make your life easier, what would you choose to invent? Why would you invent that particular gadget?"

"How might next year be a different year for you?"

"How might next year be a problem for you?"

"In what ways are you most like your mom?"

"In what ways are you most like your dad?"

"What is one thing you wish someone had told you before you got married? Why?"

"What is one thing you have never quite gotten the hang of?"

"What most causes you to become a bundle of nerves or all thumbs?"

"What is one thing you probably will never do—but would be fun if you could?"

"What are a couple of things you remember about your grandparents?"

"What does your name mean? Why were you named that?"

"What is one of the most memorable dreams you have ever had?"

"If you were going to leave the world one piece of advice before you died, what would that advice be?"

"If you were to describe yourself as a flavor, what flavor would you be?"

"What was the best gift you ever received as a child?"

"If you could raise one person from the dead, who would you raise? Why?"

"Who was one of the most interesting persons you or your family ever entertained?"

"What is the nicest thing anybody ever said about you?"

"What one thing would you like your obituary to say about you? Why?"

"What is your favorite city? Why?"

"Where do you go or what do you do when life gets too heavy for you? Why?"

"Which do you value most—sight or speech? Why?"

"When you were growing up, who was the neighborhood bully and what made that person so frightening?"

"What is your fondest memory of a picnic? Why was it so special?"

"What is the best news you have heard this week?"

"What is the worst news you have heard this week?"

"What was one of the worst things your brother or sister did to you as a child?"

"If your house were on fire, what treasured items (not talking about people) would you try to save?"

"What was your first job? What do you remember most about it?"

"Who was the best boss you ever had? What made that person so good?"

"What was your worst boss like?"

"When you were a child, what did you want to be when you grew up?"

"What did your parents want you to be?"

"If you could choose one way to do your wedding differently—like parachuting while reciting your wedding vows or holding the ceremony underwater—what would you choose?"

"Who was your hero growing up? How did you try to imitate that person?"

"What was your worst boss like?"

"What is one thing you suspect people say about you behind your back? Why do you think they say that thing about you?"

"Briefly, what was the story of your wedding day?" (If you give the members advance notice, each couple can bring their pictures to share with the group.)

"Using the following categories, what's been happening in your life lately: something old, something new, something happy, something blue?"

"In what area of your life would you like to have greater peace? Why?"

"If you could someday have a worldwide reputation for something, in what area would you like that to be? Why?"

"What is one of your biggest fears about the future?"

"What characteristics do you like best about children? Why?"

"Of the things money can buy, what do you long for the most?"

"If you had to go to prison for a year, what do you imagine would be the hardest part of that experience? Why that?"

"Who was a grade school teacher who made a big impression on you (for good or ill)? What can you tell the group about that person?"

"You have one hour with the president of the United States. What questions would you ask?" (Note that you are not looking to be political or critical here—think of questions about wisdom, decisions, challenges, and the like.)

continued on the next page

"You have been given a one-year sabbatical from work and decide to take a trip. You can't go more than one hundred fifty miles for any leg of the journey. What would you do along the way at each place you stop?"

"Break your life into three equal segments. What was the most significant event from each of those periods of time?"

Here are questions each person can answer for every other member of the group:

"Look at someone in the group. What is one aspect of that person you are glad God made that way? What does that aspect of the person mean to you?"

"What is something you have from your childhood that you'll probably never give up? Why won't you give it up?"

"What is the most useless thing you have in your house? Why is that thing still in your house—why haven't you gotten rid of it?"

"What is the one thing in your wallet (or purse) that tells the most about who you think you really are? Why that particular thing?"

"When you were a child, what was your favorite time of day? Day of the week? Time of the year? Why were these your favorites?"

"In general, what do you think people worry too much about?"

"In what area do you want to be taken most seriously?"

"What is an emotion you often feel but don't usually express?"

Remember that these kinds of questions are designed to help people open up and share *with one another.* If this becomes an "everyone answers the leader" exercise and there is no interaction between the members, do your best to deflect the responses from yourself to others. Also, remember that people will have various levels of interest in these questions, so just use what you find works the best for your group.

Facilitating Dynamic Discussions

A leader ACTS to facilitate discussions by:

- *Acknowledging everyone who speaks during a discussion.* Even if several people speak at once, make sure to recognize each one. Respond to laughter or a groan or a deep sigh. Remember, 90 percent of communication is nonverbal.

- ***Clarifying what is being said and felt.*** When someone makes a statement that needs clarifying, say, "Let me see if I understand what you are saying."
- ***Turning it back to the group as a means of generating discussion.*** Don't be the answer person. Instead, ask, "How does this discussion impact you so far?"
- ***Summarizing what has been said.*** Offer statements such as, "So far, it seems like we have been saying . . ." or "If I were to summarize the key components of the discussion so far, I would say . . ."

Questions

Another key to facilitating dynamic discussions is generating the right kinds of questions and offering appropriate responses. Here are some guidelines for the kinds of questions and responses that will help your group engage in meaningful, challenging discussions.

Opening Questions

Use an opening question to help the group members warm up to each other, allow them to get to know one another better, and let them hear their own voices. Opening questions are speculative and engaging, preparing members' minds and hearts for the topic to be discussed. You may want to broach the topic of discussion with a short, creative illustration or story that will answer the question, *Why do I want to discuss this topic tonight?* Examples of opening questions:

- "What do you look forward to as you grow older?"
- "What often drives us to fear intimacy with one another?"
- "What can we do as a group to diminish this anxiety?"

Launching Questions

Launching questions are designed to generate group interaction and feedback and get people to the goal of the discussion. They are typically designed to answer these questions: *What do I know? What do I feel? What should I do?* Examples of launching questions:

- "What do we learn from seeing the obstacles Joseph faced and how he overcame them?"
- "What do you think was going through Peter's mind at this time?"
- "After hearing tonight's discussion, it appears—and I may be wrong—that we all agree we are somewhat stuck in our conversations and it is hard to get rolling. What steps can we take to open things up a bit more?"

Some questions do not necessarily launch a discussion but solicit responses and feedback. There are two kinds of launching questions: those that are leading and those that are limiting. *Leading questions* usually produce a short answer:

- "Would you be tempted in this situation?"
- "Do you agree or disagree with this statement?"

Limiting questions indicate that you have a specific answer in mind. They do not promote much discovery, but they can help clarify facts.

- "What three commands do we find in this passage?"
- "What two things does Paul say we must do?"

Guiding Questions

Even the most well-prepared leader will need to spontaneously guide the discussion at times. Here are three ways to do this through *guided questions*:

1. ***Rephrase the question:*** "You seem to be asking, 'How can we develop trust as a group?'"
2. ***Personalize the question:*** "How would you respond to Jesus if he asked you that question?"
3. ***Test for consensus or decision:*** "Are we saying that everyone must obey this command?"

Summarizing Questions

Asking a summarizing question after a series of other questions allows you to acknowledge the group members' contributions while maintaining biblical integrity and direction. An affirming comment can be made with good eye contact and a smile by saying, "Thanks for sharing that," or "That's a good point," or "Okay, that is a response worth considering. Are there other thoughts as well?" An example of a summarizing question might be, "So what we see in this passage is that Joseph was able to see God working in his life for good even in the most trying of circumstances. Would you all agree that is correct, or are you seeing something else in the passage?"

Application Questions

The goal of the small group study is not just information but also transformation. As the leader, you can help the members apply what they have learned by asking application questions. Some examples of application questions:

- "What changes will you make this week as a result of our discussion tonight?"
- "What difference does this make to you and me?"

Responses

How you and the other members of the group respond to questions or statements will either foster or fizzle discussion. Here are some tips on how to respond appropriately to members' questions or comments.

Affirming Responses

These responses acknowledge each person's value, promoting intimacy and openness. Such responses send a strong signal to group members, telling them they have been heard, understood, and respected. Some examples:

- "Lisa, I understand this sharing is painful for you. I'm feeling very sad for the way you were treated by your boss this week."
- "Bob, I realize you want to talk, but it's important that we listen to Steven and try to come alongside him during this critical time of decision for him."

Participatory Responses

These responses invite others to join in the discussion. They not only affirm a participant's sharing but also invite others to engage in the process. Participatory responses do not isolate group members by shaming, embarrassing, or lecturing them. Some examples:

- "Susan, thank you for sharing that with us. How have others in the group dealt with the grief that you have experienced?"
- "Sam, that was a terrific insight. Could you share a bit more of how you came to that realization?"
- "Bob has shared some deep feelings tonight. How might others of you have responded to a similar confrontation at work?"

Paraphrasing or "Going Deeper" Responses

Paraphrasing responses allows you to repeat the thoughts of others and enables them to share about them more deeply. These types of responses summarize what has been shared and allows the members to explore personal feelings, thoughts, and actions. Some examples:

- "June, if I heard you correctly, I believe you stated something similar to what Keri shared last week. Do you share the same feelings as Keri on this matter?"

- "That was a very painful episode in your childhood, wasn't it, Greg? How did you deal with it? How do you face it today?"
- "It is exciting to be part of a victory like you shared, Sharon. How does that impact your relationship with your husband, Scott?"

These kinds of responses—affirming, participatory, and paraphrasing—will enable you to value your members while encouraging them to express feelings, thoughts, and personal concerns.

GROUP PRAYER

Here are some ideas on how to facilitate meaningful prayer in your group.

Model It

1. Be a person of prayer yourself. Pray for your members and for who might fill the open chair, asking God to give you his direction in leading the group.
2. When you pray out loud in the group, keep your prayers honest, authentic, and from your heart.
3. Remember these basic guidelines for group prayer:
    - Short prayers create safety.
    - Simple prayers are direct and honest.
    - Spirit-led prayers rely on God's power.
    - Silent prayers are okay for anyone, especially newcomers.

Keep It Safe

1. Don't call on someone to pray unless you've asked permission beforehand (or you know the person well).
2. Don't expect everyone to pray every time.
3. Try to avoid praying in a circle. Allow members to pray one at a time as they feel led.
4. Respect the intimacy level in the group. As the members grow in deepening relationships, a sense of safety will foster a deeper experience in prayer.
5. Be clear on who will close the prayer time.

Guide the Prayer Time

1. Give guidelines, but let the Holy Spirit lead.
2. Avoid lengthy discussions on prayer.

3. Include prayer each time you meet.
4. Use a variety of praying methods.

What Happens When Group Members Commit to Pray for One Another

1. Your relationship with Christ and with each other deepens. You experience spiritual growth.
2. There is less chance of burnout—you put problems in God's hands and trust members to his care.
3. You allow the Holy Spirit to work in your group so that your time together is filling and refreshing.
4. You see God answer your prayers in amazing ways. Your faith increases.

Creative Suggestions for Group Prayer

1. Pray through a psalm out loud together. Some examples include:
    - **Psalm 23:** Focusing on God's shepherding of us and giving us assurance in times of trouble.
    - **Psalm 27:** Expressing confidence in God.
    - **Psalm 34:** Declaring our testimonies before God with gratitude.
    - **Psalm 37:** Expressing a life of trust in God.
    - **Psalm 46:** Being still in God's presence and proclaiming we know he is God.
    - **Psalm 51:** Declaring our repentance and desire to turn and embrace God in fresh new ways.
    - **Psalm 100:** Expressing the fullness of our joy and singing before God.
2. If there are couples in the group, have spouses pray for each other.
3. Include prayer time at the beginning, middle, and closing of the meeting.
4. Pick a portion of Scripture to pray for one another during the week (for example, Colossians 1:9 or Ephesians 3:14–19).
5. Pray through specific prayer requests given in your church bulletin or program for that week.
6. If someone is in crisis, stop right then and pray for them.
7. Pray for the church, a country, a family in need, specific seeker-oriented events, or any area for which your group has a passion.
8. Do some reading about prayer. (I recommend *Praying from God's Heart* by Lee Braise and *Prayer: Finding the Heart's True Home* by Richard Foster.)

9. If there is someone in your group who has the gift of faith or encouragement, consider having that person be a prayer coordinator—someone who writes down requests each meeting and keeps track of answers. If group members have an emergency, they can call the prayer coordinator, who will notify the other members to pray for them.
10. Remember, praise can be a part of intercession. Is a member in the midst of a struggle? Have the group together praise God in the midst of the struggle (see Psalm 13).
11. If you want to cut down on the time your group spends talking about prayer requests, give everyone an index card and have them write down their prayer requests for the week. Ask them to exchange their card with the card from another member in the group. Modify this for online groups by having the members text or email their requests to another person in the group.
12. If you want to challenge your group to pray for members in the group they might not know as well, ask them to write down their prayer requests on the index card, fold the paper in half, and then put it in a hat or basket. Pass this around and have each person pick a card. Ask them to pray for the person they pick and to call that person during the week to encourage them.
13. It is important for your group members to voice their requests from God's perspective and will (John 5:14–15). So when they pray for a situation, or someone's salvation, or someone's health, or make any other kind of request, have them first stop and ask their heavenly Father, "What are your desires in this situation? What do I need to pray right now that will cause your desires to take place?"

What to Pray for Others

Intercessory prayer can be defined as asking God to act on behalf of someone else. Sometimes we don't know how to pray for our friends and family (or even those who have hurt us), yet we know we *should* pray for them. This is where Paul's words in Colossians 1:9–14, in which he gives us a pattern to follow when we pray for others, can be helpful.

Following this model, pray that the other person will . . .

- understand God's will;
- gain spiritual wisdom;
- live a life pleasing and honoring to God;
- do kind things for others;
- get to know God better and better;
- be filled with God's strength;
- endure in patience;

- stay full of Christ's joy;
- always be thankful; and
- recall God's forgiveness of their sins.

Try using this as a pattern the next time you pray and watch how God answers!

Biblical Examples and Styles of Prayer

The Lord's Prayer, which includes several kinds of petitions, serves as a basic model for all Christian prayer. There are many other prayers in Scripture that will give you a wealth of methods, or styles, for moving your group to deeper levels of praying.

KINDS OF PRAYER

Opening	"Hear our prayer."	Nehemiah 1:11; Psalm 5:1-3
Adoration	"Hallowed be your name."	Deuteronomy 10:21; 1 Chronicles 29:10–13; Psalm 34:8–9
Affirmation	"Your will be done."	Psalm 27:1; Isaiah 26:3; Romans 8:38–39
Group needs	"Give us this day . . ."	Psalm 7:1; Nehemiah 1:11; Matthew 7:7–8
Confession	"Forgive us our debts as we forgive our debtors."	Psalm 51; Matthew 18:21–22; 1 John 1:9
Renewal (protection)	"Lead us not into temptation."	1 Corinthians 10:13
Thanksgiving	"Give thanks to the Lord."	1 Chronicles 16:34; Psalm 75:1; Revelation 11:17
Blessing	"The Lord bless you and keep you."	Numbers 6:22–27; Psalm 1:1
Commissioning	"Go therefore and make disciples."	Matthew 28:18–20; Acts 1:8
Healing	"The prayer of faith will make you well."	James 5:13–16; Psalm 6:2; 41:4
Spiritual Warfare	"Get behind me, Satan."	Matthew 4:10; 16:23
Closing	"May the grace of the Lord . . ."	2 Corinthians 13:14; Ephesians 3:20–21

IDEAS FOR WORSHIP

1. Create a worship playlist and have the group listen to or sing along with it. In online settings, this works best if the technology used plays the music (and the person[s] singing) and the lyrics are posted so it is easy for the group to follow along and keep the volume steady. (See Steve Gladen's book *Small Groups with Purpose* in the Additional Resources section of chapter 7 for some great ideas.)
2. Walk through a nearby park or forest preserve and praise God for his creative power.
3. Ask your group to think of the names of God found in Scripture. Have each person tell why the name they thought of is important, and then pause as a group to give God glory for who he is. Here are some examples:

    - **Elohim:** God the creator, mighty and strong (Genesis 17:17)
    - **El Shaddai:** God almighty (Exodus 6:3)
    - **El Roi:** The God who sees (Genesis 16:13)
    - **Yahweh-Jireh:** The Lord provides (Genesis 22:14)
    - **Yahweh-Rapha:** The Lord who heals (Exodus 15:26)
    - **Yahweh-Shalom:** The Lord our peace (Judges 6:24)
    - **Yahweh-Rohi:** The Lord our shepherd (Psalm 23:1)
    - **Immanuel:** God with us (Matthew 1:23)
    - **Abba:** God our father (Romans 8:15)

4. Ask a few members to select a favorite psalm or Scripture passage that focuses on who God is or who Jesus is. Read each passage aloud and then pause to pray.
5. Have each member write prayers of worship and praise to God. Ask the members to share them with the group. Think of this as writing a letter to God.
6. Go to a worshipful Christian concert or church service together.
7. Ask the members to record images on their phones of things that cause them to think about God or want to worship him. View them together as a group. Pause to reflect on who God is and what he is doing in each of your lives.

BUILDING RELATIONSHIPS IN THE GROUP

Relationship-Building Exercises

The purpose of relationship-building exercises is to build trust and create friendships in your group by encouraging fun, communication, honesty, transparency, authenticity, and shared experiences. As relationships grow, community will be enhanced. See appendix 2 for an extensive list of relationship-building exercises. With all of these exercises, please remember the following:

- Know your goal.
- Think through the group size and break the group down into subgroups if necessary.
- Make sure you allow enough time for everyone to participate in the exercise.
- As the leader, participate alongside everyone else.
- Let the Spirit move and don't get in the way.
- Be discerning about when to step in or redirect and when to just be quiet.
- Face the awkwardness that arises as people express their emotions.

Tips for Relationship Building in Online Groups

1. Be more intentional in knowing people's names and sharing stories and details with one another. "What was your first real job? How did that go?"
2. Take advantage of sending texts and emails to communicate and follow up on discussions, prayer requests, and checking in between meetings.
3. Use icebreakers that utilize the chat function and space. For example, you could post a list of feelings and ask people to name how they are "showing up" to the meeting. Some folks use S.A.S.H.E.T. (pronounced *SASHAY*): Sad, Angry, Scared, Happy, Excited, Tender. People choose a word (or similar word), post it in the chat, and can add a brief comment as well. "I am arriving SAD today—a friend received a bad medical report."
4. Create prayer partners for the month and connect between meetings.

Social Activities

1. Eat meals together.
2. Play sports and games together.
3. Take a retreat as a group.
4. Go to a park.
5. Go to a concert.
6. Go to a lake for the day.
7. Go someplace special at Christmastime.
8. Go to a pumpkin patch at Thanksgiving.
9. Have a fall harvest party.

10. Watch a video together and critique it.
11. Make popcorn, ice cream, or pizza together.
12. Brainstorm with your group some fun things to do.

Outreach

1. Pray for someone to fill the open chairs you have in your group.
2. Pray about who you can invite to a group meeting (or to a social gathering first).
3. Pray for different parts of the world that need to hear about Christ.
4. Pray for a missionary who has been sent out by your church.
5. Plan a trip to the inner city to see needs in your community.
6. Gather materials to meet a need in your city, state, country, or in another country.
7. Have a potluck dinner and invite visitors.
8. Have a Superbowl party or Oscar night and invite neighbors.
9. Adopt a child through World Vision and support that child financially.
10. Plan to bring friends to a seeker service.

A good resource for groups who want to go deeper into outreach and sharing their faith is *Contagious Faith* by Mark Mittelberg (see the Additional Resources section in chapter 7).

CHAPTER 7

MANAGING CONFLICT IN MEETINGS

As relationships in groups deepen, conflict is inevitable. A group that experiences no conflict is probably either a brand-new group or a group that has not pursued deeper, open relationships. The following are some biblical principles for conflict management and a few conflict management strategies that you can employ as a small group leader.

BIBLICAL PRINCIPLES FOR CONFLICT MANAGEMENT

The Bible differentiates between *quarreling* and *constructive conflict*. Quarreling is negative because it refers to vain arguments or disagreements for the purpose of promoting self-worth or causing division. As James 4:1–2 states, "What causes fights and quarrels among you? Don't they come from your desires that battle within you? You desire but do not have, so you kill. You covet but you cannot get what you want, so you quarrel and fight. You do not have because you do not ask God."

This kind of quarreling is not pleasing to God. Paul told Timothy the same thing in 2 Timothy 2:24: "The Lord's servant must not be quarrelsome." However, there is much admonition in Scripture for leaders to use constructive criticism and exhortation in order to bring about spiritual growth. In 2 Timothy 3:16 this is referred to as "rebuking," and in other places as "admonition" or "exhortation."

THE DISTINCTION BETWEEN QUARRELING AND CONSTRUCTIVE CONFLICT

Quarreling (James 4:2)	Constructive Conflict (Matthew 5:23–26)
Seeks win-lose	Leads to win-win
Tends to divide and to choose sides	Seeks to reconcile and to choose steps
Exaggerates strife	Speaks truth in love
Is an end in itself	Is a means to an end
Tears down	Clears path toward something better
Usually has a hidden agenda	Is only about what is in the open
Comes from a person pushing an issue	Brought about by necessity in community
Is a battle	Is work
Is usually hard	Is usually hard

STRATEGIES FOR WORKING THROUGH CONFLICT

There are several approaches to conflict management, each of which has its own benefits. In small groups, the strategies of compromise and collaboration are probably the most effective.

Avoidance

Avoidance is the act of not addressing the conflict directly. It is an effective strategy to use when:

- the issue is trivial;
- the situation will take care of itself;
- saving face (yours or someone else's) is important; and
- time is limited.

Avoidance is not an effective strategy to use with conflict when:

- the problem is important;
- the problem will not resolve itself (and may worsen if neglected);
- credibility will be lost by avoidance; and
- there is a larger, underlying issue that is important to address.

Accommodation

Accommodation is agreeing to meet the needs or requests of the other person. It is an effective strategy to use when:

- the relationship is more important than the task;
- the issue is trivial; and
- small concessions will reap further gains (that is, choose your battles).

Accommodation is not an effective strategy to use with conflict when:

- your actions could be viewed as condescending; and
- its use would set an unwise precedent.

Compromise

Compromise is an act in which both parties agree to concede or give up something to resolve the conflict. It is an effective strategy to use when:

- there is no simple solution to the situation;
- both parties have a strong interest in different facets of the problem;
- there is not enough time for a truly collaborative solution; and
- the situation is not critical and an adequate solution is good enough.

Compromise is not an effective strategy to use with conflict when:

- a dangerous precedent will be set by failure to hold to principles or values;
- an optimal resolution is possible; and
- it is important to avoid concessions of any kind.

Collaboration

Collaboration occurs when both parties work together to bring about a solution to the conflict. It is an effective strategy to use when:

- both the task and the relationship are important;
- the time, information, and willingness to collaborate are present;
- the outcome is exceedingly important; and
- sufficient trust exists between the parties.

Collaboration is not an effective strategy to use with conflict when:

- time, trust, and resources are not available; and
- the issue is not worthy of the investment of time, energy, and resources.

CARE-FRONTING: THE CREATIVE WAY THROUGH CONFLICT

In his book *Caring Enough to Confront*, David Augsburger describes an approach to conflict management called "care-fronting."[1] The following is a synopsis of that strategy.

Incorrect Thinking About Caring

Caring is a good word when confronting is absent. There is a time for caring, and a person should care when care is called for. But caring should not be contradicted by any admixture of confrontation. To care genuinely, candor and confrontation must be forgotten, at least for the moment. When someone cares deeply about another person, it will be very difficult for them to confront that individual, because hurting that person is the last thing they want to do.

Incorrect Thinking About Confronting

Confronting is a bad word when it is compared with caring. There is a time for confronting, and a person should confront when confrontation is required. But confronting must not be contaminated by any admixture of caring. To confront powerfully, care must be laid aside. When someone is angry, they should confront. To talk of caring at a moment like that would be false.

Correct Thinking About Caring and Confronting

Together, the words *care* and *confronting* (*care-fronting*) provide the balance of love and power that lead to effective relationships. While the more common practice is to keep these distinct and separate, care-fronting offers genuine caring that welcomes, invites, and supports growth in another, offering real confrontation that calls out new insight and understanding. To confront effectively is to offer the maximum amount of useful information with the minimum amount of threat. Care-fronting unites love and power and unifies concern for relationship with concern for goals. This way, one can have something to stand for (*goals*) as well as someone to stand with (*relationship*) without sacrificing one for the other or collapsing one into another. Thus, one can love powerfully—and be powerfully loving. These are not contradictory; they are complementary.

EXPRESSING ANGER IN GROUPS

There are two ways of expressing anger in groups: "I" messages and "you" messages. "I" messages are clear and confessional. The person owns their anger, responsibility, or demands without placing blame. "You" messages, on the other hand, often take the form of attacks, criticisms, labels, devaluation of the other person, or ways of fixing blame. Encourage your group members to give clear, simple "I" messages when expressing anger.

The following are some examples of "I" and "you" messages:

"I" Messages	"You" Messages
"I am angry."	"You make me angry."
"I feel rejected."	"You're judging and rejecting me."
"I don't like the wall between us."	"You're building a wall between us."
"I don't like blaming or being blamed."	"You're blaming everything on me."
"I want the freedom to say yes or no."	"You're trying to run my life."
"I want respectful friendship with you again."	"You have to respect me or you're not my friend."

ADDITIONAL TROUBLESHOOTING TIPS

Creating safe places where life change can be maximized is not easy, and it can be reassuring to know that *all* small groups undergo some type of relational difficulty. If group members expect to grow, they will have to be vulnerable. Anyone who has ever led or been a part of a nurturing small group will tell you that where people are emotionally transparent, problems will come to the surface. When they do, it's the leader's job to help steer the group in the right direction.

Two principles should guide a leader's attempts at successful troubleshooting. First, any solution must promote the health and wholeness of the individual. Second, any solution must also promote the health and wholeness of the group. Given this, the following troubleshooting tips, which were garnered in part from discussions with seasoned small group leaders, should go a long way in helping your group to graciously and insightfully deal with problem situations.

Note that these tips for dealing with certain issues in your group were not designed to label anyone in a pejorative way. The goal is simply to identify kinds of behaviors that often arise and then find loving ways to deal with them. In this way, you can avoid breakdowns occurring among the people in your group or in the general environment—where suddenly everyone is giving their two cents and it is hard to maintain discussions.

Remember, no technique will be 100 percent successful in solving the difficulties your group may encounter. But with prayerful attention, sensitivity, and caring interaction using one or more of these tips, your group has a good chance of not only making it through your particular barrier but also realizing true community and maturity on the other side of it.

Issue #1: The Overly Talkative Member

If not moderated properly, what often begins as a trickle of friendly patter can turn into a virtual flood of words. The Talker is rarely shy and usually is uncomfortable with long periods of silence. Typically, what's behind this need to fill in the pauses is the fear of intimacy or personal disclosure. The Talker is quick to move on an item and can easily unsettle a group's pacing if there isn't some type of sensitive intervention. Here are some tools that you may find helpful.

Establish Ground Rules for Your Group

- Suggest a group guideline, such as no one should speak a second time before others have a chance to talk. (This could be especially helpful for folks who are new to small group interactions in a church setting.)
- Make (or reiterate) the guideline that no one can overrun someone else while he or she is speaking. (Translation: "No interrupting!")
- Go systematically around the group, giving each person the opportunity to talk. Remember at the onset to be sensitive with members who are either unaccustomed to speaking in a group setting or feel uncomfortable with it.
- Agree at the beginning of the meeting to save some issues for the end, after everything else has been discussed. (Note that this only works if you have seen the talkative person repeatedly focus only on certain topics.)
- One creative solution would be to pass an object around the room, and only the person holding the object has the platform to share.
- During the discussion, interject and pose a guiding question directed to another person. "Sara, as you have been processing what Dan has been sharing, what comes to mind for you? Maybe you could add some thoughts to this conversation."
- In front of the group, state that you would like to hear more about the talkative person's items of interest after the meeting.

Meet Individually with the Person

- Meet with the talkative member privately (such as after the group time ends). Tell the person you value their sharing but wish to hear other people's comments as well.
- Spend some additional one-on-one time with the person and try to ascertain the driving issues that are making it important for them to dominate the conversation. You might gently give a few examples of what you observe and what it feels like when someone takes over the conversation—and stress you want to avoid that. "For example, Kevin, when we were discussing how we model our faith at work, you . . ."

- Firmly and sensitively confront the person in private. Begin with the positive contributions the person has made in the group and the need for others to be given the opportunity to make a similar impact. Use the confrontation time as an important affirmation moment as well.
- Ask for the Talker's help in drawing others out. Suggest that the person end their comments with a question like, "So what do the rest of you think?"

Issue #2: The Answer Person

For too many years within the Christian community, knowledge has preceded action on the list of preeminent Christlike virtues. It is not hard to see, then, why many sincere members of a group see nothing wrong with throwing around easy answers, or simply quoting a Bible verse, or becoming wrapped up in some minor theological trivia that has little to do with the group discussion. These members can be argumentative and may have little tolerance for outside interpretation of feelings or biblical passages. They often will go to great lengths to make sure their opinions are heard and validated.

This excessive focus on answers can dismantle safe places. Other members should not have to experience the pain of nonattention, judgment, or an argumentative spirit. Here are some ways to provide what the Answer Person needs and keep the group process on track.

Take Action to Address the Behavior

- Before the meeting, share how pat answers or oversimplified responses make others feel. Ask the group to monitor themselves. Don't feel afraid to challenge members about this after you have set the ground rules and most members are following them.
- During the meeting, if the behavior persists and the Answer Person continues to be disruptive, backtrack to the original idea, question, or thought that was shared.
- Refocus on the passage or material being used, collect more information from everyone, and then summarize.
- Lovingly redirect the discussion to the other group members: "What do the rest of you think of this passage?" or "How do the rest of you feel?"
- Affirm what is right about the "always right" person's answers but also look for other points of view.
- Be a model of true empathy so the Answer Person can see a better way to help others.
- Remind the group of the importance of silence and active listening.
- Avoid arguing about who is right or wrong.

Meet Individually with the Person

- If this becomes a continuing problem, talk with the person outside the group. Describe to them what sharing in this manner does to the group. Speak the truth in love.
- Affirm the person for what they know, but also point out how this knowledge may not be what is needed or appropriate.
- Let the person know that they need to let other people's communication stand on its own, without judgment or immediate correction.
- Ask the member to share more feelings rather than thoughts.
- Ask the Answer Person to help summarize or rephrase points of the discussion.
- Try to find out from the person privately what drives them to always want to appear in the know.

Issue #3: The Member with an Agenda

All of us struggle from time to time with wanting to maintain inordinate control over aspects of our lives. Groups can become the arena where our sinful power struggles play out. Some individuals will repeatedly try to prove themselves by trying to redirect some facet of group life their way for no apparent reason other than their own preferences.

A person presenting this problem leaves telltale language clues. Look for phrases such as "Yes, but . . . " or "Well, I think . . . " Often this person is critical of the group process, even with items considered tabled by the group. Here are some tools to aid you in dealing with this individual.

Reaffirm Group Covenants, Values, or Ground Rules

- Have everyone in the group reaffirm, recast, reestablish, challenge, redefine (use whatever word you want) the agreed-upon guidelines for group involvement.
- Discuss these standards when everyone is all together in the group to affirm the purpose and values of the gathering.

Meet Individually with the Person

- Lovingly confront the person privately to discern the underlying problem.
- Suggest the person work with the other members to find a proactive solution that solves the problem but doesn't violate the boundary established by the group.

Issue #4: The Fix-It Member

Some folks just cannot help jumping into a discussion to solve the "problem" as they perceive it. This might be done out of a need the person has to connect a Bible verse to the situation, or the person might be making the suggestion because of their own experience. ("I remember when I struggled with that, and what I found really helped me was . . .") While the strategies used above may apply, here are some additional ideas to consider for the Fix-It member.

Redirect the Person During the Meeting

- Fix-It folks often jump in because they cannot tolerate the tension they are feeling. Instead of helping the other member process something, they offer quick solutions. Suggest a change in the process if you see this happening in your group. Say something like, "It looks like some of us are eager to help Randy, but I am not sure we heard all that he wants to share about this. So let's pause. Randy, can you tell us more?"
- As the member then shares more, ask the Fix-It person to be a sounding board, only helping the member *process* their ideas without yet offering their own.
- Later, if appropriate, you might want to bring the Fix-It person back to the situation. You might ask, "Randy, now that you've shared everything, how might we be helpful in helping you address this issue? Do you want prayer, or ideas, or people to come alongside you to brainstorm with you, or some other option?"
- If you continue to have problems with the Fix-It person repeatedly jumping in and not respecting the process, you may have to directly ask them to hold back until the person who is sharing, and the others, have had a turn to interact.

Meet Individually with the Person

- As always, if there is a time after the meeting to have a loving, truthful conversation with a repeat Fixer, choose to do so.
- Clearly offer examples of how that person's quick-fix behavior is short-circuiting the process and presuming there are simple, clear fixes that should work right away.
- Stress that what the member with the "problem" might need is just to have the space to express themselves and interact with the other group members. By offering quick solutions, the Fixer is not allowing that important interaction to take place.

Issue #5: The Member Who Avoids Challenging Discussions

When beginning new relationships, we often have a period of time in which we share facts more easily than feelings. We don't barter much in terms of emotional risk, so not much is gained at this stage. Early on, this surface-level communication is normal and shouldn't be cause for alarm.

Often, however, a group will struggle to break through the ice of superficiality and go deeper, even after many meetings. This hesitation can be the result of a leader's direction or can be caused by someone else impeding the deeper process of growth. Whatever is keeping the group in a frozen mode, you can easily prepare yourself to handle this challenge.

Determine if You Are Going Too Deep Too Fast

- Surface communication can be a sign that you are trying to go too deep too fast. So mentally take a step back to ascertain whether this is the case.
- If you sense you have moved too quickly, admit your error and be willing to proceed at a more realistic pace.
- By humbling yourself in this way, you model vulnerability rather than harming the relational chemistry of the group. Your openness works to center the group's focus and unite the participants for future growth.

Improve Your Questions

- By far, the number one way to open up a group is to lead by example. The rule of thumb is to share as deeply and openly as you would like the others to share. You set the temperature, which is especially helpful if the group is new or has new members.
- Have specific applications and questions. Don't be afraid to challenge the group.
- Ask "feeling" questions rather than just opinion or fact questions.
- When appropriate, be more directive. Sometimes ask closed-ended questions that will elicit specific answers rather than open-ended questions.
- Restate and rephrase the question. Often silence means that group members are simply unsure of what was asked of them. (Silence may also indicate that they're thinking, not that they're reluctant.)

Create a Safer Climate

- During the initial minutes of the meeting, remind the group members of confidentiality guidelines.
- Sometimes the size of the group can deter people from going deeper. Experiment with breaking into smaller subgroups if your main group is too large.
- Contact the group members outside of the meeting to see if there is anything you can do to make the questions easier to answer.

Issue #6: The Member Who Is Distracted or Doesn't Listen

Previously, we discussed the importance of having good listening skills if you want to be a good group leader. Being an active listener is key to helping guide a good discussion. It takes character as well as skills—the heart to *want* to listen and understand a person's story. This same quality is important for your group members. Even if a person is not an avid talker, it doesn't mean they are a good listener. When a member gets caught up in distractions or in their own thoughts, communication with others loses importance, the broader discussion breaks down, and the person sharing feels devalued. Here are some ways to address this problem.

- ***Model what you expect.*** Structure, like having a timekeeper or a ground rule, can help regulate the amount of sharing, especially for newer groups. But also model what you expect. For example, "As we approach our discussion time, remember that participation is invited but never demanded. As you ponder if and what you might want to share, let me go first. So . . . I was working on a project for work at home last night and got a bit frustrated . . ." You would then share at a clear and focused level to model expectations.
- ***Describe your expectations.*** As you get more comfortable with modeling what you expect, add a ground rule that describes your expectations for time, vulnerability, and creating a safe culture for listening. This might help center expectations for the group.
- ***Take time to be self-aware.*** Are you able to mirror back the ideas, words, questions, insights, and emotions expressed in the form of an interesting question? Maybe try, "Sarah, can we back up a bit? I think I heard you say that technical subjects were your favorite in high school. By your smile, I could see this was a good experience for you. Tell us how that came about."
- ***Approach the group in a way that keeps the members listening and engaged.*** Breaking up into pairs or threes allows people to share without speaking in front of ten to twelve people. Also, call people by name, affirm them, and give them a moment to ponder an answer or comment.
- ***Tune in to verbal and emotional cues to better understand the speaker.*** Invite them to ask similar questions or make observations. Get the group involved.

ADDITIONAL RESOURCES

David Augsburger, *Caring Enough to Confront* (Revell, 2009). A classic in Christian peacemaking that teaches how to build trust, cope with blame and prejudice, and be honest about anger and frustration.

J. R. Briggs, *The Art of Asking Better Questions* (Blackstone Publishing, 2025). Briggs offers a thoughtful exploration of how intentional, well-crafted questions can transform relationships, leadership, and spiritual growth.

Cindy Bunch, *The Small Group Idea Book* (InterVarsity, 2003). A resource filled with great ideas for building community, outreach, creative Bible discussions, projects, and prayer.

Bill Donahue and Russ Robinson, *Walking the Small Group Tightrope* (Zondervan, 2003). Unpacks six challenges all group leaders face as they balance the tension between good ideas and desires in groups. Provides creative strategies for guiding group members through the process of naming group realities and moving forward together to achieve group purposes.

Richard Foster, *Life with God* (HarperOne, 2010). Explores how to read the Bible for spiritual transformation, not just information.

Steve Gladen, *Small Groups with Purpose* (Baker, 2011). Using the Saddleback Church group model, Gladen describes how to lead groups that grow people in Christ. He has a solid chapter on worship in groups (chapter 9) about the basics of worship in a small group.

Roberta Hestenes, *Using the Bible in Groups* (Westminster Press, 1983). Offers creative ways to use the Bible and study it in a group setting.

Mark Mittelberg, *Contagious Faith (Course)* (HarperChristian Resources, 2021). Mittelberg introduces five approaches to evangelism—friendship-building, selfless-serving, story-sharing, reason-giving, and truth-telling—to help people deploy their natural approach to evangelism.

Note

1. David Augsburger, *Caring Enough to Confront* (Revell, 2009).

CHAPTER 8

MEASURING GROUP PROGRESS

Every ministry leader must pause and ask questions such as, "Are we really effective? Is our ministry making an impact? Are we wisely stewarding the resources God has given us? Are people growing to be more like Christ, acting as he would?" Covering this material now may seem premature, because we have not yet discussed "Caring for Members" (chapter 9) or "Impacting Your World" (chapter 10). Should we be assessing progress in those arenas of ministry as well? Of course! However, we will begin with measuring the progress of the group as a *whole* because a healthy and active group is the foundation on which many of these other areas are built.

THE VALUE OF FEEDBACK

The first thing you will need to measure your group's progress is feedback from your members. Healthy feedback solves problems and creates closeness and attachment among group members.

When your group gives feedback, it means they are confronting reality—both positive and negative. The word *confront* comes from the Latin and means "to turn your face toward." The act of giving feedback is simply your group turning their faces toward one another—and toward the truth—and asking, "What is working? What is not working? How can we make necessary changes or adjustments and do better?"

In their must-read book *Thanks for the Feedback,* Douglas Stone and Sheila Heen highlight three triggers that can hinder your ability to receive feedback from others: (1) truth triggers, (2) relationship triggers, and (3) identity triggers. First, the truth may "trigger" you if you perceive it to be unfair or judging in tone. It hurts to hear something you do not agree with or do not like to hear, so you shut down and stop listening.

Second, triggers can arise in relationships where trust is breaking down and motives are questioned. For instance, you might be okay with what another person is saying, but because it is coming *from* that person and you are not on good grounds, you will disregard any opportunities for giving and receiving feedback. You do not trust the data because you do not trust the person.

Third, when the feedback you hear challenges your sense of self or questions the quality of your work (your "identity"), you might shut down or become defensive. *You* don't feel good, so that means the *feedback* is not good.

How can you and your group navigate these triggers so you can give and receive the healthy feedback needed to measure your group's progress? The Bible provides some guidelines:

- **Psalm 15:2:** Speak truth from the heart.
- **Proverbs 15:2, 4:** Speak with knowledge and to bring healing.
- **Proverbs 15:23:** Give an apt reply and a timely word.
- **Proverbs 16:13:** Value those who speak the truth.
- **Proverbs 27:6:** Trust the "wounds" (hard words) from a friend.
- **Ephesians 4:25–29:** Put off falsehood (pretense) and speak truth.

What will be the result? Here are some benefits of feedback:

- It promotes change in behavior.
- It brings healing to relationships that might be strained.
- It solves problems caused by inappropriate behavior, such as straying from the group's vision.
- It promotes spiritual, relational, and emotional growth.
- It acts as a mirror for the truth about the group and about its members.
- It promotes wholeness in the group.
- It has a containing function—it allows you to name and address issues before they become larger problems or frustrations.
- It allows you to celebrate what is working and create strategies for doing more of those good things.

QUALITATIVE AND QUANTITATIVE MEASUREMENT

What do you measure? Items to evaluate and discuss tend to fall into two large categories: quantitative and qualitative. *Quantitative measures* include the following:

- Number of group members
- Meeting times and location
- Use of materials or study guides
- Accomplishing the mission
- How often people served outside the group

Qualitative measures deal with the feel and character of the group, whether the process is working, and how relationships are progressing. These measures tend to be more intangible, subjective, and open to a range of people's opinions. They might include:

- Relationships
- Processing disagreements or conflicts
- Prayer life of the group
- Personal growth issues
- Overall group satisfaction

You might be familiar with the qualitative and quantitative measures used in the fields of business or education. But let's take it a step further for your group. Look at these measures *in the context of where they take place—inside the circle or outside the circle*. In this way, you can get a better handle on what needs to change within the group and what needs to change as your group seeks to have impact outside the group. (This will be the focus of chapter 10.)

There are *external* and *internal* factors that can be observed to measure performance or gain feedback. Jesus understood this truth. He said that the world will know we are Christians by our love. That means love and service for one another (inside the circle) as well as for others outside the faith (outside the circle). If you look at Jesus' interaction with the apostles in the Upper Room in John 13:34–35, you will see that love for one another is the supreme measurement of discipleship. But it doesn't stop there.

Later, when Jesus prays for his followers as he heads to the cross, he describes aspects of a community that make it healthy and purposeful (see John 17:6–26). His prayer contains requests for his immediate followers (those inside the circle) and for others who will one day follow him (those outside the circle). Both kinds of requests are present.

What Is Happening *Inside* the Circle?

In your small group, there will be internal factors that require feedback and evaluation. These inner factors include, but are not limited to, the following areas:

- Quality of relationships
- Processing conflict
- Using spiritual gifts
- Meeting members' needs
- Knowing biblical truth
- Self-awareness and self-examination
- Active listening
- Healthy communication

- Effective leadership
- Shared leadership
- Staying on mission
- Logistics
- Ground rules
- Prayer and sharing

When you pay attention to these factors, the quality of group life is enhanced. It creates a healthy group environment and culture within the group that fosters authentic community.

What Kind of Impact Is Taking Place *Outside* the Circle?

It is also necessary to measure a group by what is happening externally, using questions such as:

- How are we serving others?
- How are we building relationships outside the group?
- What have we done to add new members?
- In what ways are we reaching people seeking Christ?
- Are we preparing to launch another group?
- What are the needs in the local community?

These questions are important and must be addressed. An internal focus by itself falls short of the biblical wisdom for community. It is true that much of the Bible is focused on the internal working of a biblical community. But, equally important, a healthy community is also one that engages in effective outreach and service. After all, who wants to multiply the influence of an ineffective or dysfunctional group? And what kind of impact would a group have if its members lacked character, weren't growing, and the group wasn't becoming a Christlike community? External impact is thus an indicator of group health.

Make copies of the Group Feedback and Evaluation table found on pages 145–146. Discuss additional areas for evaluation with your group, and then allow each member to fill it out. Collect the responses and then—with some refreshments to foster a conversational tone versus a tone of hard critique—discuss the results and comments together. This will be a great exercise. The key is to focus on healthy next steps and ways to improve. Make sure to celebrate what is working and commit to continuing the progress you have made in those areas.

RECEIVING FEEDBACK ABOUT YOUR LEADERSHIP

Group members not only need to provide feedback about the group but also about *you*, the leader. This may be intimidating to you (and to them), but encourage them by insisting it's a vital part of the process. Their feedback will help you lead them well! Use the followng questions to prompt this kind of feedback. (Make a copy of this list and pass it out to the members.)

LEADERSHIP FEEDBACK QUESTIONS

1. What experiences with the leader outside the regular meeting times have been especially valuable to you?

2. What aspects of the leader's life do you most need (or want) to observe so you can see a godly example?

3. What steps could your leader take, beyond guiding the regular group meetings, to help you grow? (Be specific.)

4. Comment on the leader in the following areas:

    - Availability outside of group times

- Approachability and concern

- Accountability and being firm, if necessary

- Sensitivity and compassion

5. Is there any other feedback you would like to give the leader?

6. Are there issues that are unresolved or require attention?

7. What affirmation can you give to the leader—what aspect of the whole small group experience has been especially meaningful to you?

8. How will you pray for the leader?

How Often Should You Have a Feedback Session?

About every six months (or three to four months if you meet weekly), have the group devote an extended amount of time, about thirty to forty-five minutes, to evaluating its progress. On the next pages, you will find some tools to help you plan that kind of meeting. The key is to provide a climate of safety in which you discuss progress, name reality, give grace, and make changes *together* to improve personal growth, authentic community, and group effectiveness.

What Do You Do with the Results?

Once everyone has filled out the Group Feedback and Evaluation table and you've had a group discussion, do the following to process the results:

1. Make sure everyone is clear on what needs to change and what can be celebrated.
2. Prioritize the next steps or changes, focusing on smaller items that can have a big impact. For example, in the area of logistics, the group might want to change the time or day of meeting. This is not a big deal, but it might help with issues such as attendance, childcare schedules, and work commitments.
3. Ask each member (or teams of members) to tackle a given issue. Don't try to tackle them all yourself! Assign proposed changes or improvements to others. Ask them to clearly identify the issue and to come back next meeting with a proposal for improvement.
4. The group can then engage with the proposal and, after some discussion, decide what works best and how to make the change.
5. Affirm the process. Remind members how healthy this is for the group.
6. Set a date or time frame for doing this again (in six months, for example) so that it's a regular and normal part of your community.
7. Have a group check-in every four to six meetings. This is a five- to ten-minute discussion at the end of a meeting to simply identify any sticking points, any areas for clarification and growth, any needed midcourse corrections in vision or mission, or any other modifications that might improve overall group effectiveness. Doing this between your extended feedback sessions will make those sessions more focused and less dramatic.

SHARING RESULTS WITH YOUR CHURCH LEADERS

Asking others for feedback—and then sharing that feedback with your church leadership—takes character and courage. I highly recommend it! Sadly, few people actually do this.

GROUP FEEDBACK AND EVALUATION

Inside the Circle			
	What's Working—and Why?	*What's Not Working—and Why?*	*What Are the Changes or Next Steps?*
Quality of Relationships			
Processing Conflict			
Using Spiritual Gifts			
Meeting Members' Needs			
Knowing Biblical Truth			
Self-Awareness and Self-Examination			
Active Listening			
Healthy Communication			
Effective Leadership			
Shared Leadership			
Staying on Mission			
Logistics			
Ground Rules			
Prayer and Sharing			

Outside the Circle			
	What's Working—and Why?	*What's Not Working—and Why?*	*What Are the Changes or Next Steps?*
Serving Others			
Building Relationships			
Inviting New People			
Meeting Spiritual Seekers			
Launching a New Leader or New Group			
Discovering Needs in the Local Community			

Results from Group Discussion

But asking staff members (or others who support you as a leader) to look at your completed feedback forms will show that you want to grow. It will give those individuals the information they need to provide you with focused training, resources, and information to help you lead well.

Your supporters and supervisors might already have a form or a process for giving you their feedback. If not, sharing your group's feedback with them will generate a good discussion and prompt them to be more intentional about giving you leadership feedback. You can also give the questions on page 148 to the group or to your ministry leadership as a way of generating specific feedback.

WHAT IF THE FEEDBACK IS NEGATIVE?

Sometimes we get news that we don't want to hear. An X-ray shows a spot; an annual review at work reveals that our boss is dissatisfied with our performance; a close friend or dating partner pulls away or wants to end the relationship. "Negative" results feel awful in the moment, but they may be exactly what we need to hear to grow spiritually and in our leadership.

I remember my first review at the bank where I worked after college. I sat in a chair, the office door closed, and my supervisor explained everything I had not done to build the business. It didn't matter that he had provided no clear goals for me to pursue. He had assumed that our training department (from which I was the top graduate, making this worse) had told me exactly what to do in my new role. But that department had not.

The reality was that my supervisor did not like what I was doing. It hurt to hear that, especially after twelve months of receiving strong feedback and praise. It was emotionally awkward (though I held in the pain and anger) and professionally embarrassing. But one thing it did do: It set a benchmark and context for a robust conversation about what was working and what was not. That review redefined our relationship, clarified my work objectives, and provided me with an opportunity to grow in character and skills.

What did I do that allowed me to move from a defensive posture to a proactive one? From an attitude of "That's not fair! You don't understand! Why didn't you tell me you wanted me to work in region X and on project Y?" to "Can we discuss what is expected in my role, how you want me to achieve those objectives, and what kind of relationship we need to build so I am fulfilling your expectations and the goals of the bank?"

I did these four items:

1. **Clarify reality.** First, I made sure that I had heard the feedback clearly. Our defensive posture and desire for self-justification will often keep us from listening to the truth (we will view some of it as inaccurate).
2. **Take time to think it through.** I took a day or so to mull over the review and then scheduled another meeting with my boss. I described my view of reality without being defensive, and it helped him understand my working style and strategy. Group members will appreciate that you took time to read through their feedback or think through verbal comments. It shows that you care and are willing to do some self-evaluation.
3. **Tell others what you plan to do with the information.** I acknowledged what I had heard and said I would set a time to work with my boss on a new strategy.

In your small group, let the members know that you want to make changes based on their feedback. You took it to heart, thought it through, and have adjusted some things for the future.

4. **Ask for help.** I told my boss what I needed and expected from him. I needed clarity, some resources, and some mentoring from him in areas I was not exposed to in the training process. In the same way, tell the whole group or specific members what you need from them. In many cases, they will eagerly help and take responsibility for their part in making the group succeed.

REFLECTION

- How do I react to evaluation?
- Do I get defensive? If so, why?
- Do I become apprehensive? What is my fear?
- Do I see the evaluation as an opportunity for growth?
- What help do I need in order to process any negative feedback that I might receive?
- Do I need to find a mentor?
- Do I need assistance from other group leaders? Do I need the help of a pastor?

Remember, feedback is your friend! You need it, the group needs it, and the ministry deserves it.

ADDITIONAL RESOURCES

Henry Cloud, Bill Donahue, and John Townsend, *Making Your Small Group Work* (Zondervan, 2012). This training guide helps groups become effective and includes group check-ins so they can evaluate and measure growth. Includes teaching, dramas, and creative ideas.

Bill Donahue and Russ Robinson, *Building a Life-Changing Small Group Ministry* (Zondervan, 2012). Uses seven strategic areas of focus for evaluating group life across the church and also talks about group health and quality.

Mary Schaller and John Crilly, *The 9 Arts of Spiritual Conversations* (Tyndale, 2016). Mary and John focus on nine arts but make a more unique contribution to the arts of noticing, welcoming, facilitation, and sharing, which are great skills for small group leaders to master.

Douglas Stone and Sheila Heen, *Thanks for the Feedback* (Penguin Books, 2015). This resource identifies triggers and obstacles so your group members can break them down and provide healthy feedback to one another.

CHAPTER 9

CARING FOR MEMBERS

Once you begin having meetings, developing relationships, engaging in the community-building process, and experiencing growth, you will be positioned to care for and support your group members. Your role in this is to become an encourager and caregiver, creating a caring environment in the group so you don't have to carry that burden alone.

The most rewarding ministry in small group life is caring for people as you help them move toward full devotion to Christ and face the challenges that cause pain and suffering. Your group will become a safe and loving place for people as they face these struggles and challenges. Group members will remember these loving, defining moments of care and support for many years.

This chapter is focused on intentional encouragement and responsive care. You will also find tips for responding to care needs that are beyond the group's ability to handle.

ENCOURAGING GROUP MEMBERS

Encouragement takes place when your tender love meets a member's rising fear.

Everyone has fears, disappointments, or confusion in life. Encouragement is showing others that we truly love them in the midst of their pain. In Proverbs 18:21, we read that "the tongue has the power of death and life." Encouraging words bring life; shaming or harsh words bring death. Your job is to bring words of life to people who are feeling the sting of death emotionally. Listen to the instructions of Paul in Ephesians 4:29: "Do not let any unwholesome talk come out of your mouths, but only what is helpful for building others up according to their needs, that it may benefit those who listen."

Mutual encouragement fosters an environment of authentic community.

Tips for Becoming an Encourager

- **Be slow to speak** (Proverbs 12:18; 13:3; James 1:19). A great way to encourage members is to listen to their stories with attentiveness and caring. Don't try to fix things quickly or offer glib answers to their problems or issues. Simply listen.
- **Exercise sensitivity.** The Bible reminds us that our speech should be "seasoned with salt" (Colossians 4:6). Our words should be filled with grace (Ephesians 4:29) and should mimic those of Jesus, who came in grace and truth (John 1:14).
- **Show kindness when you speak.** Words of gentleness are soothing and tender. Truth doesn't always have to be delivered from a rifle barrel. Truth spoken gently is more readily heard and more easily obeyed.

Pitfalls to Avoid When Giving Encouragement

- **Defensiveness:** As you seek to encourage others, some people might push back, saying, "You don't understand my situation!" When this happens, don't try to justify yourself. Simply listen to what they are saying and try to clarify what is being said.
- **Sarcasm and criticism:** Sometimes people use humor to lighten the load or bring relief. As a leader, you might even use it to relieve tension and bring encouragement in the form of laughter. But sometimes humor gets out of hand and becomes biting sarcasm or hurtful criticism. Remember that people are easily wounded with words (Proverbs 15:4).
- **Correction:** Don't tell others their feelings are wrong, or inaccurate, or say to them, "You shouldn't feel that way!" or "I know just how you feel." The point is, they *do* feel that way, and you do *not* know exactly how they feel. You need to instead listen carefully to determine *why* they have the feelings they are experiencing.
- **Advice giving:** Avoid giving answers before asking discerning questions (Proverbs 18:13). Advice giving can be patronizing and shut down communication. Quick advice often ignores the real problem or presumes to know quick answers to deep questions.

Engage in Active Listening

Remember, real encouragement requires active listening. It means fully engaging with another person and participating in their pain and frustration. As you listen carefully, you will be able to bring words of encouragement, comfort, and hope to the people in your group. The Bible is full of exhortations and commands to build up and encourage one another with words. Proverbs 15–18 alone provides a wealth of wisdom about the mouth, words, and the tongue. Reflect on how you might incorporate some of these truths into your group's lifestyle.

CARING FOR MEMBERS WHO ARE NOT IN PERSON

Utilize technology to reach out to those members who need care. Set up a rotating prayer schedule to make sure everyone gets a connection (especially those who are sick, needy, or in the hospital). Have each member partner with another person in the group for a month or a quarter to check in with each other consistently. Set up a Facebook page (or something similar) where members can post needs, make prayer requests, or provide other updates.

(Keep in mind that a volunteer will need to manage the page.) If a member is absent from the group and unable to attend in person, they can call or "Facetime in" to another member when the group meets to give an update—and the group can pray for them right away.

ENCOURAGEMENT EXERCISE

In chapter 6, I gave you a number of activities and ideas that can help your group members build relationships and encourage one another. Here is another. During your meeting, ask one or two group members to complete the following sentence for one or two other designated members:

> "[Name], I am so glad you are in this group because . . ."

You can do this exercise at various meetings until your group has involved every member. This also works well at a group retreat or extended gathering, where you would have the time required to involve every member (which would be difficult at a typical group meeting).

As each member completes the sentence, they should consider the other person's character qualities, actions, contribution to the group, gifts or talents, or simply the reason why they enjoy that person's presence in the group. The key is honesty and providing encouragement, not hype or merely general "everything will be fine" affirmations.

PROVIDING CARE TO MEMBERS

Giving care is part of the role of being a shepherd. God expects you, as the leader of your group, to give the same kind of care that he himself would give to his flock. This is clear from Ezekiel 34:1–16, in which God rebukes the shepherds of Israel for not giving appropriate care to their flock. As you study this passage, you see that God desires shepherds to:

- feed the flock;
- lead them to rest;
- seek the lost;

- bring back the scattered;
- bind up the broken; and
- strengthen the sick.

Being a shepherd is a serious and meaningful responsibility. That is why it's important to share the care ministry with other members (and particularly apprentice leaders). If you have too many people to care for, you will eventually burn out. But this raises the question: How much care do you provide—and how often? There are three levels of *fundamental* caregiving: personal care, mutual care, and backup care. Each is discussed in the following section. Crisis or *emergency* caregiving is covered in the next main section, "Handling a Crisis."

Levels of Fundamental Care

Personal Care

Personal care is the direct support a group leader is expected to provide for group members. Such care includes prayer support, phone calls, emails or texts, encouragement, visits during times of illness, and finding resources to help meet needs. You shouldn't have to provide such care to *every* member; the goal is to share this duty. There will be times when you might be the first (or only) nonfamily member or friend who can meet the care needs of a group member.

PERSONAL CARE CONSIDERATIONS

1. Are you the best person to provide care to this member?
2. How can you provide care without creating a dependency in which the person relies on you as the only or primary caregiver?
3. In what ways can you model caregiving for other group members so they can emulate some of what you do?
4. Which of the following caregiving approaches is the most comfortable to you, and where do you need to grow in your skills or delegate to others?

    - Personal visit
    - Email/text
    - Setting up and facilitating a group chat
    - Handwritten note or letter

continued on the next page

- Phone call
- Visiting with a partner (apprentice leader or another group member)
- Inviting the person to your home
- Meeting the person at church

Mutual Care

Mutual care is the kind that group members give to one another. It is not possible (or expected) for a small group leader to provide all the care for all the members of the group. Rather, it is the goal of a small group to provide mutual, interactive care for one another. This kind of care includes taking meals to families who are experiencing a crisis (like an illness) or a life change (like a newborn baby), visiting people in the hospital, praying with them, and assisting them with other needs. Such care enables you to fulfill the commandment that Paul sets out in Galatians 6:2: "Carry each other's burdens, and in this way you will fulfill the law of Christ."

MUTUAL CARE

1. Who in the group is most likely to share their care needs with you?
2. What care roles, such as in the list below, can you assign from time to time? (Think of each member in the group and jot down how they might best provide care to others.)
   - Praying
   - Providing meals
   - Listening
   - Providing financial or other resources
   - Visiting
   - Creating a prayer chain
   - Setting up a webpage/group chat to provide updates and post needs

Backup Care

Backup care is the support you receive to care for members. Your first line of defense should be provided by your ministry leader or staff support. In some cases, this will be a coach or other volunteer who is responsible to care for and support you and the members. If your coach is unavailable, contact your pastor or other church leader or a ministry leader. Together, work out a care strategy for the particular need you are seeking to meet. In some cases, a pastoral counselor or professional will be needed to meet the need and provide guidance.

Larger churches may have a care ministry designated to provide support in times of crisis or when a group is overwhelmed by the scope of the need (for example, the death of a close family member). You should make it your responsibility to discover *now*—not later—who is the best person or team to contact about intense or emergency care needs.

Points to Consider When Caring for People in Pain

Pain Presents You with an Opportunity for Growth

C. S. Lewis wrote in *The Problem of Pain*, "God whispers to us in our pleasures, speaks in our conscience, but shouts in our pains. It is his megaphone to rouse a deaf world."[1] Pain—whether emotional, physical, or spiritual—has a way of capturing our attention, often to the point where we can think of little else. And, yes, pain provides an opportunity for us to become better or bitter—depending on our response. But as leaders, it is not our responsibility to make others feel better, and we must be careful to not preach premature "victory messages" to those in pain.

The opportunity for growth is as real as the experience of pain, grief, or loss. As we mature in Christ, we are able to thank God—as Christians have through the centuries—for lessons that only pain can teach us (like humility, trust, or patience). We also discover a certain bond to Christ, the suffering servant, when we share in his sufferings on earth. If we are able to receive this gift, we are able to say with Paul, "I will boast all the more gladly about my weaknesses, so that Christ's power may rest on me. That is why, for Christ's sake, I delight in weaknesses, in insults, in hardships, in persecutions, in difficulties. For when I am weak, then I am strong" (2 Corinthians 12:9–10). This is not easily said . . . but true nonetheless.

Hurting People Value Your Presence over Your Words or Skills

Paul instructed believers in Christ to "rejoice with those who rejoice; mourn with those who mourn" (Romans 12:15). Here is the truth: There is little you can do or say—no magic wand you can wave—to relieve the pain of others. But you can be present with them in their mourning. You can walk with them, just as Jesus walks with each of us in our pain.

Your first response may be to want to *do* something. But what most people in pain actually want first is your love, acceptance, and presence. They want you to sit with them at the funeral, wait with them in the hospital, cry with them at the bedside of their illness-stricken loved one. These should be the acts of a leader when members suffer.

Shared Pain Is Often a Gateway

Shared pain is often a gateway to community and small group growth. When we bring our pain into community, we find deeper love, grace, hope, and healing. It seems the more people who are present with us, carrying our burdens with us (Galatians 6:2), the more we experience mercy and hope. Groups that suffer together mature together. So ask yourself . . . *Is there someone in your small group who needs a pain partner right now?*

PROVIDING CARE

1. What is your greatest concern as you think of your responsibility to provide care?
2. Which of the following actions would you consider taking to express care or concern to group members when they need help?
    - Seeking the support of elders or staff members
    - Sharing the need (with permission) with other groups or leaders
    - Sharing the need (with permission) with other care ministries in the church

HANDLING A CRISIS

From time to time in a small group, an emergency or crisis may occur. In such moments, the members will look to you, the leader, for guidance on how to handle the crisis.

In Cases of Impending Physical Danger

When there is an immediate or impending physical danger to yourself or your group members, contact the police immediately. Such crises would include:

- Life-threatening situations
- Severe accidents or emergencies
- An attempted suicide or threatened suicide
- Present threats of violence by a person to themselves or to others
- Dangerous or illegal behavior by group members (sexual assault, selling drugs, and so on)

Although you may never experience any of these in the context of a group meeting (or even with members of your group in other contexts), it is important to be aware of the possibility and know to contact the authorities immediately. Also, be sure to check with your pastoral staff person on this, as each state in the US, and country in the world, has different laws regarding your responsibility to report illegal behavior and to whom it should be reported.

In Other Serious Situations

If you have a serious situation that requires help and guidance (for example, child abuse or neglect or spousal abuse), contact your coach or church staff member *immediately* for aid in discerning the severity of the crisis and for assistance in reporting the incident to the proper authorities. Remember, in most situations, your first point of contact should be your ministry leadership. But if there is any threat of violence or danger, call the authorities immediately.

SUPPORTING VERSUS COUNSELING

As a small group leader, you are expected to provide support and encouragement to members of your group. However, you are not trained to be a professional counselor, so you should not assume such a role. Instead, your responsibility is to provide opportunities for your members to receive the care they need. Situations that may require professional help include:

- Serious marriage problems
- History of past abuse
- Addictions
- Severe personality disorders
- Mental disorders or dysfunctions

If you encounter anything that resembles the examples above, contact your coach, ministry team leader, or pastor to see what steps to take. Together, you can make a plan for encouraging the group member to get counseling or whatever form of help is needed. Note that you should never give a member's name out directly to a church leader—in such cases, it is imperative that you not violate the person's right to confidentiality. Always ask the person first for permission to mention their name if that is needed.

Keep in mind that just because you think someone is in *need* of counseling does not mean that person will be willing to *get* counseling. Work with your coach or ministry leaders to determine how to best approach an individual with the suggestion of counseling or other help.

Sometimes, your attempts to get members the help and care they need will not be readily received. They may even outright reject your desire to provide care. If you have not already experienced this, you will. It is a hard thing to fathom—you see a need, try to act and express love, but the person appears to have a hard heart and rejects you.

Here are some suggestions for what to do when this occurs.

- The Bible says to seek peace with all people (Romans 12:18; James 3:17; Hebrews 12:14), so don't push your help on the person.
- Challenge the person lovingly. Ask them to let you help. Remind the person that the body of Christ works best when everyone helps one another.
- Ask the person, "How can we help?" It's possible you misunderstood the need or offered the wrong kind of help.
- Ask the person why they are rejecting legitimate help that is obviously needed. Is it fear, pride, shame, or something else that is in the way?
- Ask if you can at least pray for the person. That's always a start. If the person rejects even that, say you will still pray for them in your private prayer time.

Remember, you are probably not a psychologist, nor can you peer into a person's soul—only God can do that. So do what you can, offer what you can, don't be afraid to gently challenge or ask why help is being rejected, and then leave the person in God's hands.

ADDITIONAL RESOURCES

William Backus, *Telling Each Other the Truth* (Bethany House, 2006). As the title implies, this resource offers guidelines for speaking the truth to each other in love, especially when the truth is hard to communicate.

Larry Crabb, *Shattered Dreams* (Waterbrook, 2010). Acknowledges that pain and suffering are real and must be embraced in community.

Lawrence Crabb and Dan B. Allender, *Encouragement* (Zondervan, 1990). A classic book on how to build into the heart and lives of others.

Shaunti Feldhahn and James Sells, *When Hurting People Come to Church* (Tyndale Refresh, 2025). Based on national research, this book shows how those in the church can bring help bring healing to the hurting and take the load off the all-too-busy pastor or lay leader.

John Ortberg, *Everybody's Normal Till You Get to Know Them* (Zondervan, 2003). Creatively describes what relationships look like, including the challenging aspects of working with people.

K. J. Ramsey, *This Too Shall Last* (Zondervan, 2020). Explores what it means to suffer and how we can encounter the grace of God that enters the middle of our stories.

Bill Search, *The Essential Guide for Small Group Leaders* (CTI Publishing, 2021). Bill provides great ideas in chapter 8 of his book to help people connect and build community in online settings.

Note

1. C. S. Lewis, *The Problem of Pain* (HarperOne, 2001).

CHAPTER 10

IMPACTING YOUR WORLD

Behind the vision "no one stands alone" are several desires for group life in the church:

- **No one grows alone.** It takes a community of Christ followers to help each person grow in faith.
- **No one suffers alone.** A caring, loving community provides resources and support in times of crisis and need.
- **No one serves alone.** There is power in numbers, and a group can accomplish so much more than any one member can when there is a project to complete.
- **No one seeks alone:** When people join together to investigate the claims of Christ, they impact each other with their stories and lives.

Since we have already addressed the first two desires, in this chapter we will address the last two desires: (1) Learn to support one another as you serve the needs in the world around you; and (2) Discover how to create a place where new people—especially non-Christians—can find a place in community. In each of these ways, your group can have lasting, profound impact in the lives of others.

As you serve people and invite people into community, your group will grow. If you have been investing in the development of an apprentice or two, you will have the capacity to care for new members as the group adds people.

GOD WANTS TO GROW HIS COMMUNITY

By inviting others to join your group, and by training your apprentice, you are creating an environment for multiplication. Since the beginning of time, it has been God's desire to create a people who would have fellowship—*koinonia*—with him for all eternity. Though he enjoyed perfect fellowship as a tri-unity (Father, Son, and Holy Spirit), he wanted to expand that community to all who put their faith in him. From Genesis to Revelation, we see God's heart in reaching people and including them in this new community:

- God's covenant with Noah (Genesis 9:8–17).
- God's promise to Abraham to make him a great nation (Genesis 12:1–5).
- God's promise to make the Israelites his people (Exodus 6:7).
- God's promise to David of an eternal kingdom and a place for the people of Israel to dwell (2 Samuel 7:1–17).
- God's desire to be known among all nations of the earth (Psalm 67).

- God's invitation for all to come and be part of his community (Isaiah 55:1–3).
- God's will to be known among all nations of the earth (Zephaniah 3:8–10, 20).
- Jesus' invitation for all to come and receive him (Matthew 11:28–30).
- Jesus' command to make disciples of all nations (Matthew 28:18–20).
- Jesus' promise that the Holy Spirit will enable all believers to witness to the ends of the earth for him (Acts 1:8).
- God's desire for believers in Christ to bring the "good news" of the gospel to the world (Romans 10:14–15).
- God's promise that all who believe in Christ will become part of a new community through the Holy Spirit (1 Corinthians 12:13).

God's desire to invite people into his community is evident in the life of Jesus, who built relationships with people like Mary (of Bethany), Martha, Lazarus, Nicodemus, the woman at the well, and the twelve disciples. This invitation to join him in relationship continues today. Just as Andrew invited Peter to follow Christ, Barnabas introduced Paul to a fledgling church, and Paul reached out to Timothy as he built churches and expanded the ministry, so God is calling people today to invite and bring people into fellowship with him and with each other.

A LONGING FOR COMMUNITY

Part of discipleship is reaching out to people who are not involved in biblical community. This includes seekers, fringe Christians, and committed believers who are seeking fellowship. Younger generations, in particular, have a desire to connect as part of serving opportunities with others. For this reason, they tend to respond better to a personal invitation (like for dinner or coffee) than a programmed mass outreach or teaching event. Their longing for community transcends the desire for more content—a move toward the relational rather than the rational.

INVITING OTHERS TO EXPERIENCE GROUP LIFE

Maybe you are asking, "How do I connect new people to our group?" Here are some steps to think through that will help you brainstorm people who could potentially be added to your group.

Step 1: Before You Invite New Members

1. Involve everyone in the small group in the process. Every member should consider how to invite someone to the group.
2. Teach the group to provide a "seat at the table" for someone. Discuss what that means—how the group can provide a safe, caring environment.
3. Regularly pray for God to bring people into the group.
4. Develop a list of potential members.

Step 2: When You Consider Inviting New Members

1. Allow potential members to meet other members of the group before they ever attend a group meeting.
2. Seek to develop relationships between potential members and other members of the group before the potential members attend a regular group meeting.
3. Allow potential members to attend a few social gatherings or other "connection" kinds of meetings before participating in the group.
4. Explain the vision of your group to potential members and ask their thoughts about it.
5. Ask potential members to think about and pray about joining the group.

FINDING POTENTIAL MEMBERS

Using the following categories, jot down names of people with whom you already have relationships or with whom you could build relationships.

Faith. People who are disconnected from your church:

Family. People in your immediate or extended family:

Friends. Your friends and the friends of other members of your group:

Firm. People with whom you work or do business:

Step 3: After New Members Attend the Group

1. Affirm new members and the people who brought them.
2. Have everyone briefly retell stories about their journey into the group.
3. Celebrate what is happening in your group with God and in people's lives.
4. Reaffirm or revise (with input from new members) group values, covenant, and/or ground rules.
5. Allow the group to deepen relationships with the new members and grow together for a season before inviting additional people.

This last item is just a broad guideline. No one wants to stifle growth, but a revolving door of people in and out of a small group of eight to twelve can be a bit disruptive. So first add new people and help them get connected and settled into the group. Also, keep in mind this is a general process for inviting people to groups. Consult your ministry leaders to determine whether all the components of this process apply to your particular kind of group. (For example, seeker or explorer groups might use a different process for inviting non-Christians into a group, and a task-oriented group may have specific guidelines that relate to accomplishing the task.)

CONVERSATIONS WITH PROSPECTIVE MEMBERS

Getting to know someone in a short time requires focus and skill. Even those who make a living meeting other people will tell you it takes time to make a connection and build trust. In a small group situation, success often hinges on a leader's ability to help a potential member find common ground with other members so they will feel at home in the new group. You will need to ask questions in order to do this and build relationships. The kinds of questions that foster friendship based on common ground can be grouped into four broad areas:

1. Background
2. Job and family
3. Interests and hobbies
4. Spiritual interests

Some example questions are given on pages 168–169. As you meet with a potential member one on one or with other group members, don't feel pressured to use all of them.

Just pick the ones you feel comfortable with or that best suit your needs. You might even want to write your own or rephrase these examples into your own words.

Note the design and progression of these questions. Direct inquiries into spiritual specifics or a person's walk with God can be threatening. Consequently, ask the simple, nonthreatening questions first. This will loosen up the person—and will probably loosen *you* up too!

As the conversation flows, mentally note what you are feeling as well as what the person is saying. Their body posture, tone of voice, facial expressions, or glances at a spouse can help you see if there is a connection or if the conversation is awkward for the person. Don't make judgments too quickly or neglect really hearing what is said. Seek to understand and find a connection that can become the first step toward a group relationship.

When it comes to online groups, remember that the connection process will be a bit different because of the unique elements of online relationships and dynamics. Many online groups keep a Facebook page (or similar kind of tool) and ask the members to post their information and key life facts (such as their jobs and family details). It is helpful if someone volunteers to manage the page, ensure security, and help the group stay informed about study topics, new members, relational opportunities, and other announcements.

Also, establish a pattern of setting aside time to introduce a new member. It is important to let the existing members know this introduction will be part of the next meeting when it occurs. Instruct them to be welcoming, ask "easy" questions, and be prepared to provide a brief but friendly description of themselves as they greet the new member.

EXAMPLE QUESTIONS

Church Background

1. How did you happen to come to this church and/or group?
2. Where did you go to church before coming here?
3. Are you from the area? Where did you go to school?
4. What was your church background growing up?

Job and Family

1. What do you do for a living? What did you do before your current job?
2. Do you enjoy your current position? If not, what's your dream job?
3. What's your schedule like? How busy are you with your job?

4. How long have you been married? Do you have any children? If so, how many?
5. As you think of your most valued relationships, what makes them important and rewarding?
6. Tell us about your extended family. Do you see your parents much? How many brothers and sisters do you have?

Interests and Hobbies

1. What do you like to do with your free time? Do you have any hobbies?
2. What do you like to do when you go out?
3. What do you do to relax?
4. Is there any new sport, activity, or hobby you would like to learn?

Spiritual Interests

1. Have you ever been in a small group before, here or at another church? If so, what did you enjoy about it?
2. Why are you interested in joining a small group?
3. How are things going spiritually in your relationship with God?
4. What do you think you can bring to the lives of others in the small group?
5. What are your expectations for the group? What do you want to see accomplished?
6. Where do you hope to be spiritually when our time together as a group is finished?

INVITING SPIRITUAL SEEKERS TO GROUPS

Some groups are not prepared to receive people with spiritual questions. At particular stages, either the nature of the material being studied or the personalities and experiences of the members can prohibit the group from effectively welcoming seekers. Given this, if your group desires to open up to seekers, you may want to work with your ministry leadership to help prepare your group for this process. In particular, you would want to be sensitive in the following areas when inviting seekers to a group meeting or a social event:

- Focus on the needs of the seeker, not on your personal agenda.
- If you discuss a Bible passage, use a translation that is seeker friendly (such as *The Message* or the New International Version).
- Stay away from religious lingo or clichés (such as "Hallelujah," "Amen, brother," "Lamb of God," or "I'm just trusting in the Blood"). Such terminology will be unfamiliar and awkward to seekers and might scare them away.
- Focus on relevance. Don't get too caught up in theological arguments or distinctions. Stick with the basic truths of Scripture.
- Allow seekers to make comments that appear strong or opinionated without judging them or attacking the content. Don't argue with them. Thank them for their input and help the group respect their questions or point of view. Listen more than you talk!
- Keep prayers simple. Use normal, conversational language when speaking to God. Help a seeker see that prayer is simply talking with God and not some religious ritual that requires special jargon.
- Don't shy away from hard issues or places where even believers have doubts. Be honest. Be truthful. Don't be afraid of speaking biblical truth—just be sure to allow dialogue and explain unfamiliar Bible terms or concepts.

These are just a few tips to give you an idea of sensitivities you need to have toward seekers. Some seekers might fit better in a seeker-targeted small group because of the nature of their questions. Many will feel welcome in a typical group. But before inviting seekers to any type of group, devise a strategy that will best serve the seeker and the members.

LAUNCHING A NEW GROUP FROM YOUR GROUP

Considerations in Launching

Some churches have models that include training an apprentice within an existing group and launching a new group from the existing group. If you or your church wants to use this approach, here are some considerations that will help you think through your strategy.

- Cast a vision for a new group from the onset of your group.
- Include this goal in your ground rules or covenant.
- Prepare your apprentice for group leadership (see chapter 4).

- Help the members understand that one purpose of the group is to give life to new groups.
- Help the group catch a vision for reaching those who are not yet in Christian community.
- Several months before launching a new group, break into subgroups for part of the meeting and have the apprentice lead one of those groups. Breaking into subgroups will allow the members to feel the process of separation from other members or from the apprentice. The goal is not to divide the group but to give some structure to the new group that is forming. (It is likely you will want to grow to fourteen to sixteen members before considering this process.)
- Seek new apprentices in preparation for the launch and ask your apprentice leader to do the same. Have these new apprentices work with one of the subgroups.
- Begin meeting as two groups for most of the meeting time.
- At the time of launch, celebrate the beginning of a new group.

Note that in online settings, breakout rooms can be helpful for starting smaller conversations and establishing relational connections that will help people explore the potential in forming a new group.

Launching Strategies

The chart on page 172 presents four ways of launching groups from an existing group.

Communicating the Gospel in Launching

Reaching out to new people is exciting and will often involve conversations with those who do not yet know Christ. The following are some helpful suggestions for sharing the gospel story. Although evangelism is not the goal of a relationship ("The only reason why I care about you is because I think you might become a follower of Christ"), engaging in spiritual conversations with people is a call of the gospel. It is the privilege, calling, and opportunity for every believer to invite those who don't know Jesus to be their Savior and friend.

Evangelism Should Be Natural

Scripture is clear that you don't need the gift of evangelism to be an effective communicator of the faith. Paul encouraged Timothy and the members of the church in Ephesus to "do the work of an evangelist" (2 Timothy 4:5). Once you understand your style of evangelism, you will be more effective at doing that work. Your style may vary from that of

LAUNCHING NEW GROUPS

	Original Group	New Group
Leader Launches New Group	Apprentice becomes leader. Finds new apprentice. Same members.	Original leader leaves. Finds new apprentice. Finds new members.
Apprentice Launches New Group	Leader stays. Finds new apprentice. Same members.	Apprentice leaves, becomes new leader. Finds new apprentice. Finds new members.
Core Group Launches New Group	Leader stays. Finds new apprentice. Some members stay. Some new members added.	Apprentice leaves, becomes new leader. Finds new apprentice. Some members follow. Finds additional new members.
"Turbo"— All Members Launch New Groups	All members are apprentices who start a new group individually or in pairs. Leader starts new group.	Apprentice becomes new leader. Finds new apprentice. Finds new members.
		Apprentice becomes new leader. Finds new apprentice. Finds new members.
		Apprentice becomes new leader. Finds new apprentice. Finds new members.

someone else, but the responsibility rests with you. Whether you use a confrontational style, an intellectual style, a relational style, or any other kind of style, remember to be natural and be yourself.

Evangelism Is Relational

Most of us need to build relationships with people prior to sharing the gospel with them. So begin developing friendships with people who are not in a relationship with God. Develop authentic relationships with friends and acquaintances.

Evangelism Is Verbal

In Romans 10:14, Paul asks, "How, then, can they call on the one they have not believed in? And how can they believe in the one of whom they have not heard? And how can they hear without someone preaching to them?" Ultimately, you will want to share about Christ in a conversation in which you communicate the facts of the Christian gospel through your personal testimony, the reading of Scripture, or some other method that works for you and connects with them.

Evangelism Is Team-Oriented

Personal evangelism is effective, but there is also strength, help, and a diversity of interaction when a group is involved in leading someone to faith. I remember a friend who decided to follow Christ while in our group. His comment later was, "I watched how all of you lived your lives, not just what you said. That was very powerful."

Effective evangelism often includes inviting people to events and gatherings that clarify the gospel or demonstrate the love of Christ. Your church has likely mobilized resources to create such environments for events and gatherings. You need not share your faith alone! Use your church's resources to help people hear the gospel in a variety of forms and presentations. Include others in praying for people with whom you have spiritual conversations.

REFLECTION

Who in the group needs help or skill training in order to become more effective in evangelistic relationships and conversations?

continued on the next page

Who do you or the group members know who is gifted or experienced in this area? (You will want to invite that person to come to a group meeting to help you all grow in your awareness, skills, and compassion for people outside the body of Christ.)

A CHRIST-CENTERED SPIRITUAL CONVERSATION (JOHN 4)

A good example of a conversation with a seeker can be found in Jesus' interaction with the Samaritan woman at the well in John 4. When you read through this scene, certain principles become obvious. Although Christ shared the gospel in different ways with different people, it serves as a basic example of a loving yet direct conversation with someone who has spiritual interests.

Note that every evangelistic conversation and process is different, so what follows is not necessarily a model of what to do—it's an example to follow. There are some things you can learn from it. Also look at other encounters Jesus had such as with the rich young ruler in Luke 18:18–30, Nicodemus in John 3, and the Pharisees in John 8:12–30. There is no formula given or set number of steps to follow. This doesn't mean that some methods we use today aren't helpful; it simply means we start with the person, not just a process.

Here are some insights from John 4.

Jesus Is Culturally Relevant (verses 1–8)

Jesus is culturally relevant. He is willing to cross social barriers and take risks.

- *Speak their language.* Jesus asks the woman for a drink of water. In that culture, water was an important topic of discussion.
- *Discover a felt need or point of mutual interest.* This woman was lonely and ashamed of her life. She was also looking for water at a time of day when, because of the heat, no one usually went to the well.

Jesus Piques Her Curiosity (verses 9–10)

Jesus piques the woman's curiosity by asking good questions and listening.

- *Ask good questions.* Jesus was interested in the woman as a person and what she was thinking and saying. He didn't rush into "closing the sale" with her.
- *Don't always be the one talking.* In a sense, Jesus asked, "What do you think living water is?" Seekers are turned off by people who have all the answers, so listen to them and give them an opportunity to talk about their concerns.

Jesus Creates Interest (verses 11–12)

Jesus creates interest by addressing the woman's deepest needs. The issue at stake is the person of Jesus Christ. The woman was focused on her needs (in this case, water), so Jesus found common ground in this area of need (water) and used it to build a bridge. Bridge building is key to the development of any trusting relationship.

Jesus Offers the Solution (verses 13–15)

Jesus offers to meet the woman's need by turning the discussion toward himself (living water and life) as the solution to her spiritual problem (the spiritual dryness and thirst of a soul disconnected from him). At this point, she is still focused on her felt need and is living a life in fear, shame, and sin. She's had many relationships, probably mostly out of fear. (In the ancient world, a woman living alone was likely to live in extreme poverty and isolation.)

Jesus Reveals that He is the Messiah (verses 16–26)

Jesus' conversation leads to a discussion of the true nature of God and to the woman having a personal encounter with the Messiah and the life he offers. We do the same when we invite someone to follow Jesus and talk about life with the living God. The Holy Spirit does the work of illumination (opening the person's eyes to truth) and transformation of the heart takes place. The person recognizes Jesus as the Savior (the Messiah) and chooses to follow him.

Jesus Invites Followers (verses 24–26, 39–42)

Jesus wants people to become followers, not religious people.

- *Follow Jesus.* When Jesus reveals himself as the true Messiah and Savior, the woman follows him and leads others to this amazing person.

- *Be a true worshiper of God.* Jesus says that "worshipers must worship in the Spirit and in truth" (verse 24). Being a true worshiper is living in a relationship with God, not following a set of rules.

IMPORTANT VERSES FOR EVANGELISM

Here are a few other key passages of Scripture that relate to evangelism.

God Desires a Personal Relationship with Us

- "Jesus declared, 'I am the bread of life. Whoever comes to me will never go hungry, and whoever believes in me will never be thirsty'" (John 6:35).
- "Whoever believes in me, as Scripture has said, rivers of living water will flow from within them" (John 7:38).
- "The thief comes only to steal and kill and destroy; I have come that they may have life, and have it to the full" (John 10:10).

Sin Keeps Us from a Personal Relationship with God

- "All have sinned and fall short of the glory of God" (Romans 3:23).
- "The wages of sin is death, but the gift of God is eternal life in Christ Jesus our Lord" (Romans 6:23).

We Must Receive Jesus and Place Our Faith in Him

- "To all who did receive him, to those who believed in his name, he gave the right to become children of God" (John 1:12).
- "If you declare with your mouth, 'Jesus is Lord,' and believe in your heart that God raised him from the dead, you will be saved" (Romans 10:9).
- "It is by grace you have been saved, through faith—and this is not from yourselves, it is the gift of God—not by works, so that no one can boast" (Ephesians 2:8–9).

Eternal Life Comes from Faith in Christ

"This is the testimony: God has given us eternal life, and this life is in his Son. Whoever has the Son has life; whoever does not have the Son of God does not have life. I write these things to you who believe in the name of the Son of God so that you may know that you have eternal life" (1 John 5:11–13).

REFLECTION

What are the opportunities for your group to reach out to non-Christians through relationships, acts of service, and strategic gatherings?

Relationships. Who can you be praying for?

Acts of service. Who can you serve?

Strategic gatherings. What can you design, or what is happening in your church, that you can leverage for connecting with non-Christians?

SERVING OTHERS OUTSIDE THE GROUP

Reaching out beyond the group involves inviting people into community, sharing the gospel with them, and serving those in need. Every group member who seeks to follow Christ is called to serve others in obedience to the gospel and by using their gifts. There are three primary ways to do this: (1) serve one another *inside* the group; (2) serve *individually*, supported by the group; and (3) serve others *as a group*. We covered the first item in previous chapters, so here we will focus on just the latter two methods for serving.

Serve Individually, Supported by the Group

It is difficult for many groups to serve together as a unit. Work schedules, family commitments, illnesses, and other conflicts can prevent total attendance at serving opportunities. Individual service (or service with a couple other members from the group) is much easier to coordinate and celebrate. However, a group can serve as a catalyst for empowering members for service. Here are a few items to consider to help your members move toward a serving lifestyle.

1. Use the Bible to Teach About Serving

A few key verses include:

- **Proverbs 22:29:** "Do you see someone skilled in their work? They will serve before kings; they will not serve before officials of low rank."
- **Mark 10:45:** "Even the Son of Man did not come to be served, but to serve, and to give his life as a ransom for many."
- **Luke 22:26:** "The greatest among you should be like the youngest, and the one who rules like the one who serves."
- **John 12:26:** "Whoever serves me must follow me; and where I am, my servant also will be. My Father will honor the one who serves me."
- **Romans 12:6–8:** "We have different gifts, according to the grace given to each of us. If your gift is prophesying, then prophesy in accordance with your faith; if it is serving, then serve; if it is teaching, then teach; if it is to encourage, then give encouragement; if it is giving, then give generously; if it is to lead, do it diligently; if it is to show mercy, do it cheerfully."
- **Galatians 5:13:** "You, my brothers and sisters, were called to be free. But do not use your freedom to indulge the flesh; rather, serve one another humbly in love."
- **1 Timothy 3:13:** "Those who have served well gain an excellent standing and great assurance in their faith in Christ Jesus."
- **1 Peter 4:10:** "Each of you should use whatever gift you have received to serve others, as faithful stewards of God's grace in its various forms."
- **1 Peter 5:2:** "Be shepherds of God's flock that is under your care, watching over them—not because you must, but because you are willing, as God wants you to be; not pursuing dishonest gain, but eager to serve."

2. Model a Servant Lifestyle

Remember that Jesus came to serve and not be served (Mark 10:45). He gave up prestige and position and even refused to exercise some of his power in order to serve others as God in the flesh (Philippians 2:5–11). So asking, "How may I help you?" is the posture that every leader should have toward group members and toward others.

3. Help Members to Serve

Help members discover their gifts, wisdom, and experience in order to serve others. Encourage them to try a variety of ministry opportunities through the church, through other groups, or simply as needs arise through personal interactions.

4. Share Serving Experiences

When you gather as a group, share what individual members have been doing as a means of motivating one another to serve.

5. Brainstorm New Ideas

Research needs in your local community. Find opportunities to help single mothers, the poor, the homeless, families with sons and daughters in the military or in harm's way, and so on. Look for people in need of home repairs, businesses to serve, social agencies to partner with, and the like.

Serve As a Group

Here are some ways to serve together that you can discuss and explore as a group.

1. Serve Together Monthly

Commit as a group that once a month, you will help at a local soup kitchen, serve at a food pantry, tutor some kids, help at a local school, or do other acts of service.

2. Put a Date or Two on the Calendar

If you cannot create a regular rhythm, identify some dates the entire group can set aside. Make sure everyone knows this is a commitment. If you are serving with a group or agency, you must show up! Don't let them plan for ten of you to come for five hours only to have five of you come for three hours. Honor your commitments! Note that this is the biggest complaint people have about those who volunteer to serve—volunteers checking out at the last minute because of a conflict (and often not a serious one but just something that came up as an inconvenience).

3. Rotate the Members

Serve as a group but rotate the members. The members take responsibility for regularly serving and promise that a set number of people (three or four, for example) will always be there. All members of the group are trained and able to serve, but it is not the same people going each time. In this way, a group can own a meaningful serving project or effort, always fulfill the commitment, and involve every member of the group over a period of time.

A LIFESTYLE OF SERVING

In closing, remember the key to service is a lifestyle of service in your group members. Sometimes this will be structured, sometimes it will be a personal, and sometimes it will be a group response to a need (immediate or otherwise). If your group is on mission with its values and commitments, service will soon become a way of life, not simply an occasional event.

ADDITIONAL RESOURCES

Scott Boren, *Missional Small Groups* (Baker Books, 2010). Shows how your group can make a difference in the world, truly impact the culture, and look outside its own needs.

John Burke, *No Perfect People Allowed* (Zondervan, 2005). Looks at the five barriers that emerging generations face as they view church culture. This is a great tool to help your group understand people in their twenties and thirties and why they think Christianity is out of touch with reality.

Rick Howerton, *Cracking the Volunteer Code* (Rick Howerton, 2026). Rick describes how to recruit, identify, train, and empower servant volunteers in the church.

Rebecca Pippert, *Out of the Saltshaker and into the World* (IVP Press, 1999). This is another great book about how to be salt and light in the world in order to impact people with the gospel as a way of life, not just isolated discussions.

Charles F. Stanley, *Developing a Servant's Heart* (HarperChristian Resources, 2020). Dr. Stanley teaches that believers are called and equipped by God to serve others selflessly. Through a practical, Bible-based study format, the book helps readers cultivate a mindset of humility and apply principles of service in everyday life.

APPENDIX 1

COMMON CATEGORIES OF SMALL GROUPS

	Life-Stage Based	Need Based	Task/Mission Based	Interest Based	Geography Based
Examples of Groups in This Category	Couples', families', men's, singles', women's	Recovery groups, grief support, postabortion	Food pantry, greeters, vocal teams, mission teams	Sports, computers, seekers, bikers	Families, neighbors, others in location
Curriculum	Chosen by leader/group	Specified by staff	Chosen by leader/group	Chosen by leader/group	Chosen by leader/group
Typical Lifespan of Group	2–3 years; many continue longer	Usually 9 weeks; can be repeated	As long as task is needed	1–2 years; many continue longer	1–2 years; based on people moving in and out of area
Meeting Frequency	2–3 times per month	Usually weekly	Usually weekly	2 times per month	Informally (ad hoc) or formally (weekly with meal)
Open Group	Yes, for entire lifespan of group	No, groups close after third week	Yes, but depends on nature of task	Yes, for entire lifespan of group	Yes; varies on group mobility
Seekers Welcome	Yes	Yes	Yes (except staff teams, elders, etc.)	Yes	Yes (depends on model)
Typical Focus	Community, study, prayer	Healing, comfort, connection	Service, community, prayer	Connection, community, study	Relational, 101/201 level discussion, serving community
Role of Leader	Connect people to community	Provide a safe place in a crisis	Complete the task and care for members	Connect people to community	Facilitator of content and connection
Group Multiplication	Usually every 24 months; if apprentice is ready	Not usually—group lasts only 9 weeks	As often as task may demand and if apprentice is ready	As appropriate; if apprentice is ready	As appropriate; starts in new areas and geographies

APPENDIX 2

RELATIONSHIP-BUILDING EXERCISES

These exercises or "guided experiences" are designed to help members engage with each other, nurturing joy, celebration, and a deeper intimacy between members overall. Most can be adapted for use in both in-person and online groups. Use your discernment as you decide the best ones to use in particular settings. Pay particular attention to your group members' ages (there are many variations across Busters, Boomers, Millennials, and Gen X and Z), makeup (all men, all women, ethnic commonalities), backgrounds, stages of life, and cultural factors.

ICEBREAKER EXERCISES

These relationship-building exercises are designed to help the members introduce themselves to one another and get to know a bit more about each other at a personal level.

Other-Person Introductions

When introductions are needed, instead of everyone introducing themselves, ask each person to introduce someone else in the group. If it's a couples' group, have the spouses introduce each other. This can be very affirming.

Hot Seat

Before your meeting, write down some questions on individual pieces of paper (one question on each piece of paper) and put the papers in a pile. Call each group member, one at a time, to sit on a seat in the room, facing everyone. Have this person on the "hot seat" choose a question from a pile and answer it. For the next three to four minutes, invite members in the group to pose follow-up questions or discuss the person's responses. Sample questions might include:

- "What is your favorite book of the Bible? Why?"
- "How would you finish this sentence: 'Lately, I am becoming more . . .'"
- "How would you complete this sentence: 'The feeling that best describes where I'm at right now in life is . . .'"
- "If there were one person in the world whom you could spend a day with, who would that person be? Why that person?"

Questions in a Hat

Before your meeting, fill a hat (or bowl) with opener questions on individual pieces of paper (one question on each piece of paper). Have at least as many questions as there are people in the group. Vary the depth of the questions so they are appropriate for your group. Add the following special instructions on separate pieces of paper and put them in the hat:

- "Pass to the right"
- "Pass to the left"
- "Boomerang (back to you)"

At the beginning, state that everyone always has the right to pass on any question (to put people at ease so they don't feel put on the spot). Someone, let's say "Mary," picks a question out of the hat. Mary can ask anyone in the room (but only one person) to answer that question. Say she asks "John." After John answers the question, he picks a question and asks it to anyone in the room *except* Mary, and so on.

If a member pulls one of the papers with the special instructions, they can save it and use it when someone asks them a question. If they use a "Pass to the right," then the person on their right must answer the question. If they use a "Pass to the left," then the person on their left must answer the question. If they pull a "Boomerang," then the person who asked them the question must answer it. (Of course, anyone can pass at any time if they wish.)

Three Material Possessions

Ask the group members to imagine they have just discovered a major fire in their home. Assuming they have gotten their family and pets safely out, what three *material* possessions would they take with them from their burning home? Have the members explain why they would take the items they chose. Then generate a discussion to discover the value behind each of these possessions and why they hold those certain items so dear.

Two Truths and One Lie

Give everyone in the group a sheet of paper and a pen or marker or ask them to use their phones. Have them list two true things about themselves and one lie. These can be in any order. Read the list and see who can guess the lie. The person then explains why each item is a truth or a lie.

It's a Wonderful Life

In advance, secretly ask three close friends (you may include the spouse) of each group member to write out what the world would be like if that person had never been born. Before reading these aloud, cue up the scene from the classic Christmas movie *It's a Wonderful Life* where George Bailey tells the angel, Clarence, it would be better if he had never lived. After viewing the clip, read one of the three letters aloud for each person. Allow time for the group to comment. (*Note*: This may take two meetings. Keep it to five minutes per member.)

Photo Sharing

Have the group members share one image on their phones with the group. Have them explain what was happening in that moment and why they wanted to capture it.

Picture of the Group

The purpose of this exercise is to have each member take a "picture" of the group—but not on their phones. Instead, have each person make a drawing or use a word picture to describe what the group looks like. For example, they might describe the group in these ways:

- **A hospital:** A place where wounds are healed.
- **A gas station:** A place to be refueled spiritually.
- **A fortress:** A safe place where struggles can be shared.
- **A debate team:** A place where they can wrestle with differences of opinion.
- **A sports team:** A place they work together to accomplish a goal.
- **A mountaintop:** A place to gain perspective and be encouraged.
- **A carnival:** A place for fun, enthusiasm, and excitement.

These are just some examples, but have the members either draw or describe the kind of group environment they see.

PERSONAL SHARING EXERCISES

These exercises are designed for the group members to go a bit deeper by sharing about themselves to the others at a more personal level.

Break It Up

If your group is large enough, break it up into smaller groups (even pairs) for this activity (or use breakout groups if you are meeting online). Have the members spend two to three minutes sharing something about themselves with the other person, or they can pray together. This exercise is especially useful in allowing relationships to deepen.

Fill in the Blank

Ask various members of the group to complete the following statements:

- "Something I will most likely take for granted tomorrow is . . ."
- "Last year at this time, I never would have thought that God would . . ."
- "The person I am most thankful for this year is . . . because that person . . ."
- "One specific attribute of God that I most appreciate is that he is . . ."
- "The people God used to enrich my life this past year are . . ."
- "I want to thank the Lord for giving me the gift of . . . so I can use it to serve him and the church."
- "Considering the standard of living of most of the world's population, I am rich because I have these material blessings . . ."
- "If I could stand up and shout anything to the rest of the body of Christ tonight, I would tell them that . . ."
- "My God is . . ."

Gauges

Ask people to check how they are doing with their lives as represented by these five gauges:

1. **Emotional:** *How am I feeling emotionally? Strong? Fragile? Frustrated?*
2. **Relational:** *What is the quality of my family relationships and friendships?*
3. **Physical and Recreational:** *Am I healthy? Am I having any fun?*
4. **Ministry Fulfillment:** *What is my joy level in places I serve or ministry teams I am a part of?*
5. **Spiritual:** *How might I describe my relationship with God these days?*

Life Story

Over a period of several weeks, have each member of your small group spend fifteen minutes telling their life story. Then allow fifteen minutes for discussion and interaction. The point of the exercise is to find out exactly where people have come from. Often it's hard to appreciate people until we understand their past and some of the significant events in their lives.

Time Line of Your Life

Distribute paper, pens, or markers, or have the group do this exercise on their phones. Ask each group member to draw a timeline of their life, showing three to five major life events on that line. (The number of events can vary, depending on how much time you have during your meeting.) Then let each member briefly explain what they drew. (Note this exercise won't be as applicable to online groups unless the members share their timelines with others ahead of time.)

Attributes of God

Ask each person, "What attribute of God has been especially meaningful to you lately?" (For example, "I really appreciate God's faithfulness to me because . . .") Have the person talk about this, and then share your input as well. As a variation, don't just *talk* about this attribute of God but go right to prayer and praise God for having that trait.

Your Name in a Verse

Pick a topic ahead of time and choose a verse or passage on that topic—one for each member of the group and one for yourself. During your prayer time, have each person read their assigned verse or passage and then, putting their name in it, pray through it. For example, imagine the topic is "God's love for us" and you chose Psalm 13:5–6 as a passage. The group member would read aloud Psalm 13:5–6 and then pray: "I, Sandy, trust in your unfailing love; my heart rejoices in your salvation. I will sing to you, Lord, for you have been good to me."

Remember When

In Scripture, we often see God's people recounting their past experiences and remembering the Lord's deeds. Your group members can do the same by recalling for the group:

- How they first heard about Christ.
- Their testimony of how they came to Christ.
- Times when God answered their prayers.
- Moments when God brought them through a difficult situation.
- If the group has been together for a while, things they have been through together and what they meant to them.
- The story of how they first came to the church and what the church has meant to them.

This exercise builds a sense of history for the group if they've been together for a while. Recounting God's character or their experiences can be a prelude to a time of worship.

SERVICE EXERCISES

These exercises are designed for the group members to build relationships by serving together.

Serve Each Other

Have the members look for opportunities to serve each other outside of the group time. This will go a long way in them developing relationships with each other. Ideas include:

- painting a room in someone's house;
- doing a large cleaning project; or
- bringing meals when help is needed.

Serving Others Together

Ask the members to look for opportunities to serve as a group, providing help, support, or encouragement to someone else. Here are a few ideas of what to do:

- Help a needy family or person(s).
- Partner with an organization in your community that helps others.
- Serve at church during a special event (for example, during the Easter service).
- Look into an international ministries opportunity.

CELEBRATION EXERCISES

These exercises are designed to help the members build relationships by celebrating the group, each other, and what God has done in their lives.

Celebrate the Group

Search for things to celebrate: the group starting, birthing, or growing; the members' personal accomplishments; the end of a season for your group; a successful experience. Be creative in the way you celebrate. Enjoy being together!

Celebrate in Worship

Ask the members to share videos for a special time of worship, praise, or singing.

Celebrate that "He Is Able"

Ask people to bring something to a meeting that represents or reminds them of how God has proven himself able to act in their lives. Keep these guidelines in mind:

- This should be something they can hold up and talk about.
- Members should talk about their own experience (not someone else's).
- The experience they relate should be something that happened recently.

At the meeting, let each person relate their story. You may then wish to close this time by asking everyone to sing or listen to the song "He Is Able." As a variation, you could also hold a "God answers prayer" celebration, asking the members to relate how God has recently answered a prayer and what that has meant to them.

Celebrate with a Communion Service

The purpose of this is to share in the bread and the cup as a small group. This can be an incredibly meaningful experience. Each person, one at a time, will personally serve another group member. (You can assign whom they will serve in advance or simply move around the circle.) As they serve each other, make appropriate comments about the love of Christ, specifically for the individual being served. When you are done, have the group close in a time of prayer and/or worship. (*Note*: You might need to check with church leaders about doing a communion practice in your groups.)

APPENDIX 3

STUDYING THE BIBLE TOGETHER

Here is a more detailed use of the "Engage and Examine" approach to reading the Bible we discussed in chapter 3. It's a more informational approach and can be used to gain insight into the original meaning of a passage. Before you follow this approach (or any other you take in encountering the Word of God), first prepare to study the Scripture by taking a moment to pause and slow down. Set aside distractions, pressures, and the temptation to plow your way quickly through the text. Next, settle into a posture that is open, receptive, humble, and willing to listen to God and others. Finally, set aside a few moments for prayer, asking the Holy Spirit to move within you and the group, teaching you as you study the Bible together.

1. PROBE

In this step, you observe and ask what the text is saying. Read the entire passage through several times. Try using several different translations (such as the NIV, NKJV, NASB, ESV, TLB, *The Message*, or *The Passion Bible*) for a fresh look at the passage each time you read it. This will help you identify key words and develop insights into the text.

Context

Next, answer the following in writing:

- Who is writing or speaking and to whom? What is their relationship?
- What is being discussed? What is happening?
- Where does the event or communication take place?
- When does this take place relative to other significant events?
- Why does the speaker say what he does? What problems were the recipients facing?
- How does this passage fit into the context? (For example, what comes before and after?) How is God using this text to speak to you?

Structure

Examine the structure of the passage and make note of any significant connecting words that help you understand the author's message (for example, *therefore*, *but*, *and*). Try to paraphrase the passage using your own words. Are there any key words that help you understand the author's emphasis?

Word Study

List all the key words in the passage. Use a Bible dictionary (either print or online format, such as *Vine's Expository Dictionary* or *Richard's Expository Dictionary of Bible Words*), or a good study Bible (such as the *NIV Study Bible*), or Bible software, or any search tools your church might recommend (such as Logos Bible Software) to understand their meaning. You do not have to make this complicated to be thorough—just start by using some basic resources.

Questions

Now write down answers to the following questions as you read the passage:

- What are the commands to obey?
- What are the promises you can trust God to keep?
- What do you learn about God? About Jesus? About the Holy Spirit?
- What do you learn about your fellow believers? The church? The world?
- Are there any repeated words, ideas, themes?
- Are there any comparisons or contrasts (for example, life in the "flesh" versus life in the "Spirit" in Romans 8)?
- Are there any lists (like the fruit of the Spirit in Galatians 5:22–23)?
- Are there any cause-and-effect relationships (such as in Romans 10:14–18)?

2. PERCEIVE

In this step, you ask what is the key message or focus of the text.

Truths

List specific points of truth from your observations of the text. Ask questions that probe its meaning. Look at each verse, recording your understanding as you ask yourself questions such as, *What does this mean? Why is it important to understand this? How did this relate to the original audience?* Look up cross-references to help you interpret the passage. Pause again to ask the Holy Spirit, your teacher, to guide you and reveal God's truth to you.

Commentaries

Consult trustworthy commentaries, resources from sound Bible institutions, or wise teachers or leaders in the church to gain their perspective on the text you are studying. Ask the people in your small group to look at the passage with you as well.

Themes

Write down in a sentence the main idea or point you think the author is trying to get across. You may want to write down two or three main principles you discovered that develop the theme.

3. PRACTICE

In this final step, you ask whether you will allow the passage to transform your life. In Matthew 7:24-27, Jesus makes an exhortation at the end of the Sermon on the Mount, his most powerful teaching to his followers on how to live life in the kingdom of God. He says that truly wise people are those who don't simply listen to his teaching but also put it into *practice*. Paul adds, "All Scripture is God-breathed and is useful for teaching, rebuking, correcting and training in righteousness" (2 Timothy 3:16). According to Paul, how do we put the Scripture into practice?

Teaching

Ask, "How will this truth change my life, my church, my family, my work?"

Reproof

Ask, "Where do I fall short? Why do I fall short?"

Correction

Ask, "What will I do about it? What will I correct? How will others help me do this?"

Training in Righteousness

Ask, "What practices, relationships, and experiences will I pursue so that I might train myself to be like Christ?"

Studying the Bible together with a solid method like this will bring forth much wisdom, knowledge, and fruit as you live it out together as a group and in your personal life.

ADDITIONAL RESOURCE

Gordon Fee and Doug Stuart, *How to Read the Bible for All It's Worth* (Zondervan, 2003). This book provides an in-depth look at the culture, genre, and literature of the Bible to help you understand the context and culture of the Bible as you read it.

ABOUT THE AUTHOR

Dr. Bill Donahue is a popular conference speaker, prolific author, and leadership consultant. He has leadership experience in both the for-profit and non-profit arenas. After working for P&G in New York and the PNC Corporation in Philadelphia, Bill became Director of Leader Development & Group Life for the Willow Creek Church and Association, where he created leadership strategies and events for more than 10,000 leaders on six continents in over thirty countries.

Bill has a bachelor's degree in psychology from Princeton University, a master's degree from Dallas Seminary, and a PhD in Adult Learning and Development from the University of North Texas. He serves as an adjunct teacher at a number of graduate schools, training both master's and doctoral students in organizational strategy, team-building, leadership development, and transformational community.

In addition to his bestselling *Leading Life-Changing Small Groups*, Bill developed the ReGroup™ training resource with Dr. Henry Cloud and Dr. John Townsend and partnered with Steve Gladen on *Building Biblical Community*. He also co-authored *Coaching Life-Changing Leaders* with Greg Bowman, has partnered with Russ Robinson to create a number of resources for strategic leadership, and collaborated with Dr. Les Parrott on *Small Group Insights*, an online assessment and learning tool for building authentic relationships in any group or team.

From the Publisher

GREAT STUDIES

ARE EVEN BETTER WHEN THEY'RE SHARED!

Help others find this study:

- Post a review at your favorite online bookseller.
- Post a picture on a social media account and share why you enjoyed it.
- Send a note to a friend who would also love it—or, better yet, go through it with them!

Thanks for helping others grow their faith!

www.ingramcontent.com/pod-product-compliance
Lightning Source LLC
LaVergne TN
LVHW031120060826
845145LV00014B/3027

* 9 7 8 0 3 1 0 1 8 3 5 6 3 *